africana woman

HER STORY THROUGH TIME

africana woman

HER STORY THROUGH TIME

Dr. Cynthia Jacobs Carter

Introduction by Dr. Dorothy Height

NATIONAL GEOGRAPHIC

WASHINGTON, D.C.

table of contents

Introduction.....8

Author's preface.....11

1 royalty.....14
    IN HER OWN WORDS   Hatshepsut.....22

2 from africa to the new world.....40
    IN HER OWN WORDS   Nancy Morejón.....58

3 out of slavery.....70
    IN HER OWN WORDS   Sojourner Truth.....86

4 making a place in the world.....98
    IN HER OWN WORDS   Ida B. Wells-Barnett.....118

5 taking society by storm.....126
    IN HER OWN WORDS   Mary Church Terrell.....138

6 speaking out.....158
    IN HER OWN WORDS   Coretta Scott King.....168

7 Leaders on the world stage.....188
    IN HER OWN WORDS   Yvonne Brathwaite Burke.....198

8 setting the pace in the new millennium.....218
    IN HER OWN WORDS   Mary Moran.....232

Africana Woman: Her Time Line.....246

Endnotes, Authors.....250

Acknowledgments, Additional reading.....251

Index.....252

Illustrations Credits.....255

Ebony skin against brilliant color in cloth and beads highlights and enhances the beauty of all. For thousands of years, African women and men have worn woven textiles and beaded jewelry as regular attire as well as a symbolic expression of cultural, religious, political, historical, familial, or personal identity.

Preceding pages: A Kikuyu woman silhouetted against the Kenyan sky evokes the timeless beauty of the Africana woman, which is echoed in women around the world—living embodiments of the African diasporas that have occurred over centuries, beginning nearly two million years ago.

DEDICATION

For my parents, Flossie J. Purnell and Charles Purnell, who inspire me daily, and for my husband, Karl Wayne Carter, Jr., who shares his love and wisdom without question or pause.

Into a daybreak that's wondrously clear
I rise
Bringing the gifts that my ancestors gave
I am the dream and the hope of the slave.
I rise
I rise
I rise

—from "Still I Rise," by Maya Angelou

INTRODUCTION

faith, hope, and love—these have sustained women of African descent from the beginning of time to the present day. They have been vital from the day the first woman left her South African homeland with family members by her side. They guided the wise women ruling Egypt and other African nations. They sustained women through the days of slavery and in the struggle for hard-earned freedom. They move us today as we face our trials and celebrate our triumphs.

Africana Woman: Her Story Through Time is an overview of women of African descent through the ages. The beauty of the book, aside from the astounding images, is that it brings together our story in one work. It shows the links between Black women whether they are African, Brazilian, Canadian, Caribbean, European, or American.

History has its own power. This is a time when we women of the African Diaspora need history's truth to challenge hateful assumptions, negative stereotypes, and distortions about our own role in human progress. It is not enough to know about the injustices and exploitation Black women have endured.

We owe it to ourselves to be reminded of the heroism of Harriet Tubman and Sojourner Truth, share the pride of Madame C. J. Walker's business acumen, and enjoy the tremendous creative artistry of a pantheon of Black women writers, performers, and thinkers. As we garner inspiration from women of the past, we gain the power to take history further and the will to use the power of history to construct a better future. The realities in this beautiful book—the photographs, the biographic sketches—promise to liberate our best for creating a better world.

Dr. Cynthia Jacobs Carter has written an important book. I am blessed to have had firsthand experience with women portrayed in this book, like Mary McLeod Bethune, Mary Church Terrell, Marian Anderson, and Sadie T. M. Alexander, to mention a few. And it is encouraging to know firsthand the contributions of women like Dovey Roundtree, Alexis Herman, Oprah Winfrey, Maya Angelou, Sheila Sisulu, and Condoleezza Rice. It is inspiring to see these women in the context of Africana history. We owe it to ourselves to learn more about the strengths, the valued traditions, the intellect, creativity, and courage of women. Indeed, Africana women have accomplished much against all odds. They have opened new paths for a greater future.

You will be thrilled with what you read here. You will see that Africana women rise to the occasion and do what is needed at the time. Women are learning more and more the importance of working together. As you read these pages, never forget the strong legacy left for us, whether by a grandmother, a mother, a mentor, or someone we have never even met. We have always had a story to write. We have tried to make the world a better place. It has never been easy, but it has always been necessary.

This book stimulates renewal of the historic strength and spirit that is the Africana woman. The legacy of Dr. Mary McLeod Bethune has been important in my life. She said to women, "We must remake the world. The task is nothing less than that." This is the imperative to fulfill the vision of Mary McLeod Bethune and countless women who came before and after her. And this book will, undoubtedly, help rekindle for us the indomitable spirit of the Africana woman.

—Dr. Dorothy Height

In her nearly 70-year career, social activist Dr. Dorothy Height has inspired millions as a prominent organizer and leader representing Black women around the world. As fourth president of the National Council of Negro Women, she set the pace for Africana women to rise to their full potential in all walks of life—and she continues to do so as president emerita and chair.

Preceding pages: An Ethiopian woman in the highlands of Welo province quietly tends to a daily chore. Photographed at home, suffused in the silvery glow of day break, she could almost have been lifted from a canvas by the Dutch painter Vermeer, whose paintings celebrated the beauty and dignity of ordinary life.

author's preface

apower unites the daughters of Africa throughout the world—a power that is drawn from the spirit of the ancestors. Through the centuries, this power has fueled Africa's daughters, creating in them a will to survive, and to thrive in the face of obstacles. Mother Africa remembers her daughters as, one by one, they appear from behind the golden curtain of time: Queen Tiye, her Nubian skin glistening in Egypt's sun, takes her throne beside her beloved husband, Pharaoh Amenhotep III. Nzinga, Queen of Angola, comes into view, leading her troops against the Portuguese. She stands victorious as Mother Africa looks on with pride. These stories and more are the beginning to this centuries-long tale.

This book is a narrative of Africana women through time. It is not a comprehensive documentary, but one that is representative of Africana: It reveals the lives of women sold into slavery in the 17th and 18th centuries, ripped by the very roots from their homeland and transported across unyielding seas in conditions of horror, to be transplanted in harsh environments around the world. And it reveals how through this all, Africana woman held fast to a life force, a strength of purpose. She persevered.

And time went by: The 19th, 20th, 21st centuries. Africana woman, whether princess or handmaiden, commanded a formidable presence. In Jamaica, Nanny, Queen of the Maroons, led rebellions against slavery. Queen Charlotte Sophia, wife of England's George III, held court with pride and dignity. In Canada, Parliament hailed Rosemary Brown as its first Black female member. In America, the Female Talented Tenth, Race Women, and others led the way: Anna Julia Cooper, Mary Church Terrell, Frances Harper, Ruby Blackburn. Today, Dorothy Height, Coretta Scott King, Ruth Simmons, Carol Moseley-Braun, and so many others continue the pace with strength, wisdom, and effectiveness.

These women and others have been the carriers of civilizations and their cultures, as well as the preservers of the folkways and mores of their people. This book seeks to recognize the roles of Africana women as curators of the past, guardians of the present, and harbingers of the future. Too many women of all races around the world remain relegated to the shadows. The Beijing Women's Conference in 1995 showed the necessity for bringing to light positive female images for every society on the globe. This book serves as a step in that direction.

—Dr. Cynthia Jacobs Carter

The attire of two women walking on Gorée Island, off Dakar, Senegal, blends harmoniously the traditional with the contemporary. Their dress serves as an expression of both personal and cultural identity. This is especially apparent in Gorée—and in many other parts of the world—where tradition still holds strong sway.

Following pages: "Put on a church hat [and] I had instant class, a bunch of class," writes fashion designer Olufemi Elom, photographed here in a favorite hat. Sunday dress has long been as significant in African-American culture as decorative beadwork and brightly patterned textiles in African culture.

In ancient times only the deities
lived in the world.
Their mother was Nananbouclou.
She hurled fire into the sky.
It remains to this day.
It is called Baiacou:
the Evening Star.

      —from an African folktale

1 Royalty

f rom the dawn of civilization, Africa's royal women have shown themselves to be intelligent, resourceful, courageous, passionate—and sometimes vulnerable. Although born and raised in different parts of the continent, they all shared a common desire to forge their own destinies and to live on in eternity. Their astounding stories, true and fabled, survive today to reveal their accomplishments and their legacies.

By 1500 B.C., Egypt's great pyramids had stood for more than ten centuries. Egypt had survived periods of plague, pestilence, and even opulence and now was enjoying a renaissance. The Hyksos—invaders from southwest Asia who had ravaged and controlled Egypt for decades—had been driven from Lower Egypt, the land encompassing the Nile River Delta and its northern valley. In addition, Egypt's armies were marching south to conquer Nubia, a fertile land that stretched along the banks of the Nile, near present-day Libya. While Egypt added new territories to its boundaries, it also grew internally—to become the undisputed center of culture and politics in the larger eastern Mediterranean world. It was the beginning of the New Kingdom—a period of great Egyptian power and wealth that would last four centuries, from around 1539 to 1070 B.C. Hatshepsut, one of Egypt's most fabled rulers, lived in the early years of this glory.

Daughter to Pharaoh Thutmose I and Queen Ahmose-Nefertere, Hatshepsut was born around 1500 B.C. Beautiful and intelligent, Hatshepsut knew a life of great wealth and privilege. When Thutmose I died around 1492 B.C., the Egyptian court insured the continuation of the royal bloodline by wedding her, a full-blooded royal, to her half-brother. Thutmose II was the new pharaoh and the son of Thutmose I by a lesser wife. (Incestuous marriages were common among Egyptian royals since the women carried

PEOPLING of the WORLD

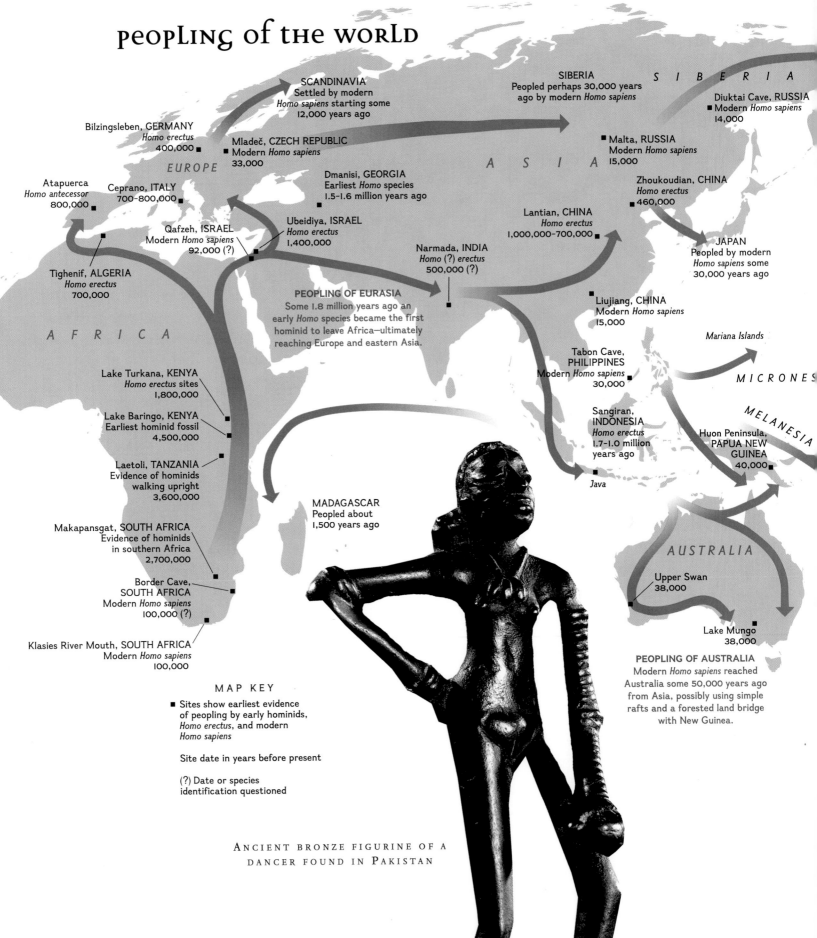

SCANDINAVIA
Settled by modern
Homo sapiens starting some
12,000 years ago

SIBERIA
Peopled perhaps 30,000 years
ago by modern *Homo sapiens*

S I B E R I A

Diuktai Cave, RUSSIA
■ Modern *Homo sapiens*
14,000

Bilzingsleben, GERMANY
Homo erectus
400,000 ■

Mladeč, CZECH REPUBLIC
■ Modern *Homo sapiens*
33,000

A S I A

Malta, RUSSIA
■ Modern *Homo sapiens*
15,000

EUROPE

Dmanisi, GEORGIA
Earliest *Homo* species
1.5-1.6 million years ago

Zhoukoudian, CHINA
Homo erectus
■ 460,000

Atapuerca
Homo antecessor
800,000 ■

Ceprano, ITALY
700-800,000 ■

Lantian, CHINA
Homo erectus
1,000,000-700,000 ■

Qafzeh, ISRAEL
Modern *Homo sapiens*
92,000 (?)

Ubeidiya, ISRAEL
Homo erectus
1,400,000

JAPAN
Peopled by modern
Homo sapiens some
30,000 years ago

Tighenif, ALGERIA
Homo erectus
700,000

Narmada, INDIA
Homo (?) *erectus*
500,000 (?)

PEOPLING OF EURASIA
Some 1.8 million years ago an
early *Homo* species became the first
hominid to leave Africa—ultimately
reaching Europe and eastern Asia.

Liujiang, CHINA
Modern *Homo sapiens*
15,000

A F R I C A

Mariana Islands

Lake Turkana, KENYA
Homo erectus sites
1,800,000

**Tabon Cave,
PHILIPPINES**
Modern *Homo sapiens*
30,000

M I C R O N E S

Lake Baringo, KENYA
Earliest hominid fossil
4,500,000

M E L A N E S I A

Laetoli, TANZANIA
Evidence of hominids
walking upright
3,600,000

**Sangiran,
INDONESIA**
Homo erectus
1.7-1.0 million
years ago

**Huon Peninsula,
PAPUA NEW
GUINEA**
40,000

MADAGASCAR
Peopled about
1,500 years ago

Java

Makapansgat, SOUTH AFRICA
Evidence of hominids
in southern Africa
2,700,000

AUSTRALIA

**Border Cave,
SOUTH AFRICA**
Modern *Homo sapiens*
100,000 (?)

Upper Swan
38,000

Klasies River Mouth, SOUTH AFRICA
Modern *Homo sapiens*
100,000

Lake Mungo
38,000

PEOPLING OF AUSTRALIA
Modern *Homo sapiens* reached
Australia some 50,000 years ago
from Asia, possibly using simple
rafts and a forested land bridge
with New Guinea.

MAP KEY

■ Sites show earliest evidence
of peopling by early hominids,
Homo erectus, and modern
Homo sapiens

Site date in years before present

(?) Date or species
identification questioned

ANCIENT BRONZE FIGURINE OF A
DANCER FOUND IN PAKISTAN

HIGH ARCTIC
Peopled about
4,500 years ago

Greenland

NORTH AMERICA

PEOPLING OF THE AMERICAS
From Siberia across Beringia came
modern *Homo sapiens* into the
New World. Most experts believe
humans had moved into North
America by 14,000 years ago, but
some isolated sites hint at peopling
20,000 years ago and earlier.

Meadowcroft, U.S.
16,000 (?)

Blackwater Draw, U.S.
11,000

HAWAIIAN ISLANDS
Peopled about
1,600 years ago

P O L Y N E S I A

PEOPLING OF THE PACIFIC
Modern *Homo sapiens* came to islands
near New Guinea perhaps 32,000 years
ago. But the rest of Melanesia—and all of
Micronesia and Polynesia—were peopled
much later, from 4,000 to 1,000 years ago.

Taima-Taima,
VENEZUELA
14,000 (?)

Guitarrero Cave,
PERU
12,000

Pikimachay, PERU
22,000 (?)

SOUTH
AMERICA

Fiji Islands

Tagua Tagua,
CHILE
11,400

Monte Verde,
CHILE
12,500

NEW ZEALAND
Peopled by Polynesians
about 1,000 years ago

STONE HEAD PORTRAYING AN
OLMEC RULER FOUND IN MEXICO

Los Toldos Cave,
ARGENTINA
12,000

Fell's Cave,
CHILE
11,000

Our earliest human ancestors
—Homo erectus—ventured
forth from Africa into Asia,
Europe, and the Middle
East about 1.8 million years
ago. Less than 100,000 years
ago, Homo sapiens, the
direct ancestors of modern
humans, began a second
migration out of Africa.
Although whether Homo
sapiens replaced or interbred
with Homo erectus is still
debated among scientists,
Africa remains the undisputed
birthplace of mankind.
Those earliest travelers are
thought to have sowed the
mitochondrial DNA for
ancient human populations
around the globe, including
Dravidians in India,
Aborigines in Australia, and
possibly the Olmec in Mexico.

19

the royal blood.) Though still a very young woman, Hatshepsut ruled as Thutmose II's principal queen.

She of Noble Bearing ... Great Royal Spouse ... Daughter of the God Amun ... First Lady of the Two Lands. Hatshepsut proudly wore these titles as queen. She stayed in the background when Thutmose sat on his throne, but her intelligence was always evident. Thutmose frequently left Hatshepsut in charge when he journeyed abroad—leading successful military campaigns into Syria and Nubia that acquired both land and great wealth. Before Thutmose II died, he named his only son—seven-year-old Thutmose III, born to a harem girl—his successor. Since Thutmose III was too young to rule on his own, the Egyptian high court designated Hatshepsut as co-regent. A wise and ambitious woman, Hatshepsut understood her position and ruled judiciously.

Although Hatshepsut could have declared war on her neighbors, she chose to focus instead on national affairs. She built education and arts facilities. She dismantled the main army and sponsored peaceful diplomatic expeditions into Punt, Asia, Greece, and strategic areas on the continent of Africa. Later, caravans and ships followed, trading in gems, ivory, ebony, oils, spices, incense, and even trees. Hatshepsut continued to rule even after Thutmose III came of age. It appears that they split the duties: She oversaw the administration while he commanded the military. A few years later, however, with Thutmose III involved in military campaigns, Hatshepsut crowned herself pharaoh.

She used to her advantage the Egyptian belief that a royal birth resulted from the union between the pharaoh's mother and Amun-Re, the supreme deity. (Some experts believe that this notion, a heavenly god fathering a human child, may have sowed the seeds for Christianity.) Hatshepsut claimed that Amun-Re had come to Queen Ahmose-Nefertere in the human form of her husband, Thutmose I. Since she, Hatshepsut, was the child of that union, she concluded that she was the rightful child to rule all of Egypt. To legitimize her claim to the title of pharaoh, she ensured that the people of Egypt recognized her as pharaoh by always appearing in public in full royal male regalia: a simple robe, red-and-white crown, royal wig, and a nems (a striped cloth placed around the wig). She also donned a false beard, facial hair being strictly forbidden to all but the pharaoh. She even claimed a pharaoh's privilege and had a burial tomb carved out for herself in the Valley of the Kings, adjacent to that of Thutmose I.

As peace thrived under Hatshepsut's reign, wealth grew. Hatshepsut spent her fortunes on monuments to the gods, both to honor them and to ensure her prominence in the afterlife. Senmut, a renowned architect and astronomer of the era—reportedly a Black

In an Algerian cave painting at least 5,000 years old, a man (second from right) joins four women in a dance ceremony that calls on the earth goddess to bless the tribe's cattle. The female figures are crowned with traditional hairstyles that resemble those worn by Fulani women today. The scene itself reflects a ceremony still practiced by the nomadic Fulani tribespeople living in the Sahel, on the southern fringe of the Sahara.

man and her lover—built several temples and obelisks upon her instruction. Today, Egypt claims many of Hatshepsut's commissions among its greatest wonders of the past. One such marvel is the large mortuary temple built of limestone at Deir el-Bahari intended to honor herself and her human father, Thutmose I. The temple steps back into the cliff in three levels, each faced by a colonnade and adorned with relief sculpture that depicts in great detail the glory of the expedition to Punt that Hatshepsut financed.

Another monument, the Red Temple at Karnak, housed the statue of Amun-Re. Each year during the Opet—a celebration honoring the new year—temple priests carried Amun-Re's statue from the Red Temple to his shrine at Luxor to receive the worship of his subjects. In return for their loyalty and offerings, Amun-Re was to shed favor upon them for the next year. Four obelisks built of red granite from Aswan and inscribed with hieroglyphics in honor of Amun-Re flanked the Red Temple. They stretched to the heavens in height and splendor, their surfaces of electrum glinting in the sun. One still stands today after 35 centuries, a hint of electrum still adorning its surface; its inscription begins:

QUEEN HATSHEPSUT (CA 1500-1458 B.C.) WORE THE GARB OF A PHARAOH.

HATSHEPSUT

This formidable ruler of Egypt's New Kingdom built
obelisks at Karnak to honor her divine father, Amun-Re.
She had them inscribed with her words, as below.

It is the King himself who says:
I declare before the folk
  who shall be in the future,
Who shall deserve the monument
  I made for my father,
Who shall speak in discussion,
Who shall look to posterity—
It was when I sat in the palace,
And thought of my maker,
That my heart led me
  to make for him
Two obelisks of electrum,
Whose summits would reach
  the heavens....

I have done this with a loving heart for my father Amun;
Initiated in his secret of the beginning,
Acquainted with his beneficent might,
I did not forget what he had ordained.
My majesty knows his divinity,
I acted under his command;
It was he who led me,
I did not plan a work without his doing.

Hatshepsut died in 1458 B.C. after effectively ruling for more than two decades. It is not known how Hatshepsut died. What is known is that despite her opulent public life, Hatshepsut may have had one secret love. Discovered in her tomb, lying beside the great ruler, was an ebony-skinned baby, mummified and wrapped in the royal tradition with Hatshepsut's insignia.

Following Hatshepsut's death, Thutmose III assumed the full role of pharaoh. Thutmose III is said to have despised his stepmother and her reported relationship with Senmut. He felt ignored and scorned by Senmut, and he believed that Hatshepsut squandered his heritage at Senmut's directive. Perhaps in retaliation, Thutmose III ordered destroyed many of Hatshepsut's creations, especially where she was depicted with Senmut. Many temples Hatshepsut had built, as well as statues of her likeness, were defaced. On some statues the royal emblem was knocked off her headdress; on others the eyes were pecked out with a small chisel. Still, Thutmose III could not completely destroy her legacy. Her monuments—and her story—endure. Written on one of the obelisks at Karnak is her enduring declaration: "As I shall be eternal like an undying star."

Several decades later, with Egypt still thriving under the influence inspired by Hatshepsut, Pharaoh Amenhotep III wed Tiye, a young Nubian of noble birth. Tiye was born around 1400 B.C.; her father Yuya served Amenhotep as a Master of Horse and Chancellor of the North. According to some historians, the introduction of Tiye into Egypt's royal family changed the fate of Egypt forever—it solidified Egypt and Nubia in a bond that brought Black Africa and North Africa together. Under Amenhotep, the kingdom stretched from the farthest tip of Egypt's New East to the Kingdom of Napata in present-day Sudan.

Amenhotep III became pharaoh around 1390 B.C. when he was 10 to 12 years old; he married Tiye, who was around the same age, shortly thereafter. He proceeded to marry many more women, forging political alliances that brought Egypt wealth and strategic military alliances. Many of his wives were of noble birth, including the daughter of the King

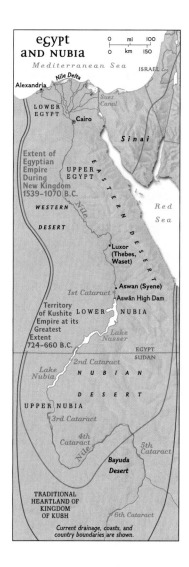

EGYPT AND NUBIA

Distinctly adorned Nubians bear tribute to their Egyptian masters in a 14th-century B.C. tomb painting (opposite) located in the Valley of the Kings. For centuries, Egypt subjugated Nubia (above), a rich and ancient land of Black Africans, to gain its gold and other treasures. But in the eighth century B.C., Nubia's Kingdom of Kush conquered Egypt, ushering in Egypt's 25th dynasty.

of Babylon; however, Tiye, with her charm and beauty, was Amenhotep's favorite wife and his principal queen. She would hold the position as the Great Royal Spouse of Amenhotep III for nearly 50 years. Because Amenhotep held Tiye in such high esteem, he proclaimed her an equal of a king—the first time a nonroyal had achieved such status. She was also the first queen depicted on even par with her husband in royal portraits.

Tiye's husband showed her his affection in many unique ways. He had her accompany him to many events, even though royal protocol called for Amenhotep's mother, the carrier of the royal bloodline, to accompany him to certain official ceremonies. (One can only imagine how his mother felt about having to share her time and the attention of the masses with her daughter-in-law from Nubian origins.) He built Tiye a gorgeous barge, the *Splendor-of-Aten*, then dug an artificial lake so she could float the craft for special ceremonies, fireworks, or whatever pleasure she desired. He also commissioned for her a great

complex of structures in western Thebes; it is believed Tiye resided in the southeast quarter of the complex in what is called the South Palace. Amenhotep went even further by erecting a splendid temple dedicated to her worship in the Nubian city of Sedeinga, on the west bank of the Nile in present-day Sudan.

Amenhotep loved and trusted Tiye so much, and so respected her intellectual capabilities, that he considered her a trusted advisor and confidante in affairs of state. He often left her in charge while he traveled on missions to increase Egypt's honor; his faith in her judgment was proven correct time and again when she ruled alone for long stints.

When Amenhotep died in 1353 B.C., Tiye's power and influence did not end as was the case for many previous queens. In fact, when Tiye's son Akhenaten (Amenhotep IV) took the throne, she became secretary of state, a position second only to the pharaoh. Leaders from other countries routinely conferred with Tiye on matters regarding international relations, remembering and respecting her earlier actions as queen to Amenhotep. Tushratta, King of Mitanni, beseeched Tiye to influence Akhenaten to honor the agreements made between himself and Amenhotep: "You are the on[e, on the other ha]nd, who knows much better than all others the things [that] we said [to one an]other. No one

A stone scarab (above) commemorates the marriage of a love-struck, teenage Amenhotep III to his beautiful Nubian queen, Tiye. A wood bust (opposite) carved many decades later shows a mature Tiye. At about the time of her husband's death, Egyptians began to worship Tiye as a goddess.

[el]se knows them (as well)." Eager to continue the goodwill between their two kingdoms, he added "You must keep on send[ing] embassies of joy, one after another. Do not cut [them] off." Tiye served as the liaison between the courts at Thebes and Amarna, Akhen-

aten's new capital. Meanwhile, Akhenaten, encouraged by his mother, preoccupied himself with religious reform, proclaiming for the first time in human history the idea of a single god. He named Aten, the solar disk and a lesser god to Amun-Re, the supreme deity. He devoted himself to his beliefs and the building of Amarna, which would be the center of worship for Aten. Tiye died around 1340 B.C., but her groundbreaking accomplishments in matters of royalty and affairs of state live on.

Just as Egypt claims Tiye as a queen, Ethiopia claims Makeda, the Queen of Sheba, as one of its own. Makeda (or Bilqis as she is known in the Islamic world) is considered by Ethiopians to be the mother of the Ethiopian royal bloodline that commenced in the tenth century B.C. and continued to modern times.

The story of Makeda is written in the Bible, the Koran, and the *Kebra Negast* (Glory of Kings, an Ethiopian epic), each with subtle variations. According to legend, Queen Makeda learned of the wisdom of Jerusalem's King Solomon from a merchant prince named Tamrin, who had been engaging in trade with that king. Old Testament scripture states in I Kings that when the Queen of Sheba heard of the fame of Solomon, she decided to prove him with hard questions. She set out to see the king, carrying with her an abundance of gold and spices. Like any visiting dignitary, Makeda did not want to arrive empty-handed. Her gifts were both an offering of peace and a demonstration of her prosperity. The Song of Solomon in the Bible has Makeda allegedly saying upon her arrival, "I am black but comely, O ye daughters of Jerusalem."

King Solomon loved women and reportedly had a harem of more than 600 wives and concubines. He was instantly struck by Makeda's beauty and wished to claim her for his own; however, the Queen of Sheba was bound to chastity. So enthralled was Solomon by the Black queen that he respected her wishes. Still, he seldom left her side. He lavished her with feasts during which the two of them dined and talked every night until dawn; he commissioned for her an apartment made of crystal and had a throne for her placed at his side. For six months Makeda witnessed his decisions, actions, and interactions with his people. Only then, as said in I Kings 10: 6-7, was she convinced of his wisdom:

> And she said to the king, It was a true report that I heard in mine own land of thy acts and of thy wisdom.
> Howbeit I believed not the words, until I came, and mine eyes had seen it: and, behold, the half was not told me: thy wisdom and prosperity exceedeth the fame which I heard.

Then, according to the *Kebra Negast*, she announced that it was time to return to Ethiopia and her people. They needed her. Her announcement saddened Solomon; he had hoped to convince her to consummate their union, for he very much desired a son born of this strong, intelligent, and beautiful woman.

The *Kebra Negast* relates that King Solomon created a situation to fulfill his dearest wish. He made Makeda's final night more festive than all the previous days and nights she had spent in Jerusalem. He lavished her with everything that his royal throne could summon. Fiercely attracted to Solomon, Makeda's resolve finally crumbled, and she welcomed the king into her bed. The next day, Solomon supposedly gave Makeda 6,000 chariots laden with gifts, and a vessel that traveled in the air. Upon returning home, Makeda learned she was carrying Solomon's child; she named him Menilek, the Son of Wisdom, to honor his father.

When Menilek reached manhood, Makeda gave him a ring and told him to seek his father in Jerusalem. The young man did as his mother requested. Legend says that Menilek spent time with his father, learning from his wisdom. Eventually the young man returned to his mother's people in Ethiopia, having been anointed a king in Jerusalem, to found the Solomonic dynasty. The wisdom and intelligence of both his parents was evident in his reign. Whether fact or fiction, Ethiopia proudly claims that the Solomonic dynasty, begun with Menilek and unbroken until the death of Haile Selassie in 1974, descends from King Solomon and the Queen of Sheba.

Hundreds of years after Hatshepsut, Tiye, and Makeda had become part of Africana history, Yennenga of West Africa came forth. According to oral histories passed down from generation to generation, Yennenga was born the daughter of King Madega

This two-inch silver amulet shows the goddess Hathor suckling the wife of Piye, Egypt's first Black Pharaoh. In this uniquely Kushite twist on traditional Egyptian iconography, a female queen rather than a male pharaoh receives divine sustenance, suggesting her great status. Five queens in succession ruled Nubia during its final years, declaring themselves "God's wives" to assert divinely ordained power.

of Dogomba, a kingdom that covered much of present-day Ghana. It is believed she lived some time between the 11th and 15th centuries.

The histories tell us of Yennenga's strength of character and loyalty to her father. She commanded her own battalion and the royal guard. Yennenga performed many heroic acts in defense of her father's kingdom, frequently fighting by her father's side. However, as she grew into a young woman she longed for more than the glory of battle. She wished for a family. She made her father aware of her feelings, yet he quickly dismissed any suitors that dared approach. Yennenga decided to chart her own destiny.

One night, dressed as a man and escorted by loyal retainers, she left home on the back of a wild stallion. The party traveled for days. Then one night, exhausted, Yennenga could go no further; she and her entourage happened upon a tent in a region peopled by the Bousanc—and stopped. Still in disguise, Yennenga accepted the hospitality of the owner. He was Raile, a Mande prince in exile from Mali, where his father had been deposed. Legend has it that Yennenga kept her true identity hidden. She stayed with Raile for days, listening to him talk about his conquests on elephant hunts. Finally, her long hair fell from under her helmet, revealing her to be a beautiful princess, not a prince as Raile had believed.

The two married and lived in his tent. A year or so later, she bore a son; the couple named him Ouedraogo—Stallion—for the horse that carried Yennenga to her husband. When Ouedraogo was 17, Yennenga took him to meet her father. Apprehensive at facing the king, Yennenga was relieved to find him elated to see her, to discover he had long forgiven her for leaving. Reunited in spirit with her father, Yennenga returned to Raile and the life she had made for herself. However, she left Ouedraogo in her father's care so he could learn all that King Madega could impart. Some time later, when Ouedraogo felt sufficiently educated, he requested permission to leave. The king then revealed to Ouedraogo that he was next in line to the throne, but this grand gesture was not enough to satisfy the son of Yennenga. Ouedraogo, much like his mother, wished to follow his own path. He desired to establish his own kingdom. The king,

determined not to make the same mistake twice, gave Ouedraogo his blessings and a large troop of men-at-arms to command.

After stopping to pay homage to his mother and his father, Ouedraogo set out to found the Mossi Kingdom. The kingdom once covered much of present-day Burkina Faso and northern Ghana, and still exists today. From the 11th century to the present, the kingdom has known only one dynasty: the descendents of Ouedraogo—a chain of 30 monarchs. By following his mother's example, Ouedraogo honored her. In legends, the Mossi Kingdom is known as the tree born of the trunk of the great warrior Yennenga. Griots (storytellers of tribal histories) sing of the young girl of 14 who rode bravely into battle on horseback, her hair floating in the wind like the mane of a lion. To this day, out of respect for Yennenga, all Mossi warriors revere the lion and refuse to kill it except in self-defense. Yennenga lives on in the many business establishments, roads, and public gardens that bear her name and in the statues that abound.

Griots farther west in West Africa tell the story of another young woman who epitomizes the strength and character of the Africana woman. In the late 1600s, Amina Kulibali, the young daughter of the new king of the Massaleke people of southeast Senegal, was chosen to marry the eldest son of the late king who had most recently ruled their land. One night, Amina's fiancé, unwilling to wait the required year for marriage, slipped into the bed of his intended. Shortly thereafter, Amina learned she was with child; filled with shame and aware of the disgrace and humiliation it would bring upon her father, she fled.

She took a few servants and many bags of gold and traveled deep into the neighboring territory of the Gambia, where many of the same tribes as those in Senegal—including the Wolof, the Serers, and the Tukulor—lived. Several months passed. Then, by chance, the heavily pregnant Amina met the king of Gabu, who thought her the most beautiful woman he had ever seen. He instantly desired her, but Amina would not again be swayed by charm. Legend says that she studied the king for some time, then declared, "If I follow you, the child who is within me will be king in the country where he will be born." The king agreed to her terms. He was so smitten that he even disbanded his other wives so that Amina would never have cause to be jealous. Amina gave birth shortly thereafter to a girl, and to be true to his word, the king said the children of this child would be his successors. These successors, among them a great ruler named Goria and his three sisters, established a kingdom between Gambia and Gsangomar.

The legendary meeting between beautiful Makeda, Queen of Sheba, and wise Solomon, King of Jerusalem, is depicted in 13th-century stained glass from France. Power, riches, and beauty were always hers, but the mother of the Ethiopian royal bloodline craved wisdom above all else, allegedly telling her people that it was "far better than treasure of gold and silver."

The king of precolonial Dahomey in West Africa leads his celebrated female warriors, called Amazons, into battle, as depicted in this 18th century painting. In another illustration (above), a lone warrior holds the decapitated head of an enemy. A European observer marveled that the Amazon women "are far superior to the men in every thing—in appearance, dress, in figure, in activity, in their performances as soldiers, and in bravery."

In the same century, but farther south, the magnificent Anna de Sousa Nzinga of Ndongo (present-day Angola) rose to prominence—first as a king's brave daughter and later as a revered warrior queen. At the time of her birth, most likely 1581, Portuguese missionaries had converted to Catholicism many of the Mbundu, the people living in and around Ndongo. A few years later, Anna's father, King Kiluanji, fearing that the Europeans would convert all of his people—destroying their heritage—banned missionaries from his country. In addition, he effectively cut off the Portuguese from the endless supply of Mbundu slaves they were taking and shipping to the Americas. The act amounted to a declaration of war, and set off years of conflict between the Portuguese and the people of Ndongo. Nzinga fought in many of the battles.

At the height of the warfare, Nzinga's father died. His kingdom was placed in the hands of Nzinga's older, illegitimate brother, Mbandi. The jealous Mbandi was aware that Nzinga commanded the respect of his counselors, as much for her diplomacy skills as for her prowess on the battlefield. Consequently he ordered Nzinga banished and her son killed. In addition, griots sing of how he ordered his women retainers to sterilize Nzinga with a sizzling hot poker. Others say that instead of a poker, they used scalding water.

A few months later, after losing battle after battle—his armies with their traditional weapons were no match for the Portuguese Army—Mbandi begged for Nzinga's help in negotiating a peace agreement with the Portuguese. She spoke their language and knew their ways. Even though Nzinga still mourned the murder of her son, and her own humiliating sterilization, she decided to come to Mbandi's aid, though for her people's sake, not his.

In 1622, she set off to Luanda, the stronghold of the Portuguese, to meet Correia de Sousa, the new Portuguese governor. She entered the city in a royal procession preceded by musicians and an honor guard of warrior women. The governor attempted to insult Nzinga by receiving her seated high on a dais in a large carved chair; he only provided her with cushions on the floor. Not one to be bested by wits, Nzinga quickly came up with an alternative. She clapped her hands and one of her retainers came forth, bowed on elbows and knees, and offered her back as the perfect chair. Nzinga brokered a settlement whereby the Ndongo kingdom would return Portuguese prisoners of war and help the Portuguese in the slave trade in return for sovereign recognition and the withdrawal of Portuguese forces from Ndongo lands. She even accepted the Jesuit faith and was baptized (taking the name Anna de Sousa); everyone in Luanda attended the grand ceremony. Although the negotiations were nominally successful, Nzinga doubted that the Portuguese would honor the accords. Her suspicions were shortly confirmed when the Portuguese did not withdraw their armed forces and confine their activities to the coast.

Realizing that Mbandi was an ineffective leader, incapable of holding off the Portuguese onslaught, Nzinga returned to Ndongo. She had her brother arrested—she perhaps even arranged his death by poison a few days later—and she assumed the throne, declaring herself queen. She ignored the Mbundu custom that strictly forbade women to take positions of power, choosing to treat it as a mere formality. To further establish herself on the throne, she gathered a harem of young men as her "wives," just as a king would gather a harem of young women for his pleasure. In a final nod to Mbandi, Nzinga also avenged her son's death by taking the life of Mbandi's son.

From the moment she took the throne, Nzinga ruled with the heart of a warrior rather than of a diplomat. Over the next 40 years she waged intermittent warfare against the Portuguese. She led her army into battle even at the age of 60. Against mounting military pressures, Nzinga retreated to neighboring Matamba in 1656; later she agreed to the peace terms offered by the Portuguese and she voluntarily returned to the Jesuit faith. But she never stopped fighting for her people. And although her people were sometimes torn in their devotion to her because of her flagrant violations of Mbundu custom, they revered her for her courage, strength, and leadership. When Nzinga died in 1663, she was celebrated just as she had lived: as a queen. She was buried in a religious habit, and draped in her pearls-and-gold-accented royal robes.

Nearly 100 years after Nzinga ruled, a shy girl named Nandi was born in the present-day KwaZulu-Natal region of southern Africa. Quiet and unassuming, she was the orphaned daughter of the chief of the Langeni people, members of the Zulu clan. One day in the late 1780s, when she was in her early teens, Nandi encountered Senzangakhoma, the chief of the Zulu. Dazzled by his presence and flattered by his attention, Nandi shunned the Zulu tradition that said there could be no union between people of the same clan. When Nandi discovered she was pregnant, Senzangakhoma took her as his third wife. The privilege of being one of the chief's wives, however, could not outweigh the dishonor and shame of their illicit intercourse. Both she and her son, Shaka, born of that forbidden union, were vilified. Life in the clan became unbearable.

When Shaka was six years old, Nandi and Senzangakhoma separated; she returned to the Langeni with Shaka. The Langeni were no more forgiving. She and Shaka met the same disapproval, but Nandi refused to flee. For the shame she had brought upon her family, she chose to bear the recriminations: humiliating tauntings and harassments. As a boy, Shaka was constantly teased and beaten by the other boys in the kingdom. In 1802, the Langeni cast out Nandi and Shaka. Eventually the Dletsheni, a subclan of the powerful Mtetwa people, gave them shelter; but they still were not safe from hateful words or actions. Nandi had finally had enough. She drew on her inner strength to rise above the injustices that had been meted out to her. She proceeded to devote her life to one pursuit: raising her son to become the greatest warrior of all time. She gave Shaka a stick and instructed him to hit those who hit or even looked at him. She would come to regret those instructions.

Shaka grew to manhood and became a warrior for the Mtetwa; he excelled on the battlefield. When Shaka turned 29, Dingiswayo, the overlord of the Mtetwa, released him from military service and sent him to take command of the then faltering Zulu clan. Using his military prowess, Shaka turned the small clan into a great nation of warriors. The Zulu nation grew through political alliances and the assimilation of clans his armies decimated. Thousands of people in neighboring clans were killed as Shaka increased the nation's territory. While many people, including his own, found him fierce and tyrannical, the Zulu nation took pride in his abilities to fight off the encroaching Europeans.

Throughout his childhood and into adulthood, Shaka had maintained a strong attachment to Nandi. Her love supported him and pushed him to the heights, yet she exerted a gentling hand. It is said that as Shaka's thirst for power and bloodshed grew, Nandi could no longer appeal to his humanity. In 1827, she died as a queen mother who had lost touch with her son, the greatest warrior of his time. Her death profoundly affected Shaka; he was consumed with grief. He ordered the entire Zulu nation to mourn Nandi's death for one year. Nandi, who had been so unassuming at birth, then commanded in death the reverence of an entire nation of warriors.

For more than a thousand years, a Yoruban queen sculpted in brass has held her noble gaze. From the ancient West African city-state of Ife, she ruled her people. Centuries later, Yorubans dispersed across the Atlantic Ocean would carry with them a legacy of respect for their powerful female ancestors.

Following pages: Life-size human figures carved during Africa's Pastoral Period decorate a sun-drenched rock face in eastern Chad. The "Beautiful Ladies," as locals call them, bear markings reminiscent of body painting still practiced in parts of Africa today.

Oh, you (who are as) the gold of
Nairobi, finely moulded,
You are the risen sun, and the
early rays of dawn.

—traditional Somalian poem
    translated by B. W. Andrzejewski
    and I. M. Lewis

2 from africa to the new world

Something of old forgotten queens
Lurks in the lithe abandon of your walk,
And something of the shackled slave
Sobs in the rhythm of your talk....

—from "To a Dark Girl,"
by Gwendolyn Bennett

When Queen Nzinga of Ndongo handed over prisoners to the Portuguese in the 1600s, she, like countless other African monarchs and heads of state, profited by exchanging human lives for trade goods. The Portuguese and other merchants from Europe specialized in "Black Ivory"—Africans, most destined for sale in the New World. The transatlantic slave trade—or the triangular trade, as it is also known—exchanged European goods for Africans, who were then sold in the Americas for sugar and the like, which was then sold in Europe.

As early as the mid-1400s, Portuguese traders took Africans to Spain, Portugal, and other European countries to sell as servants or laborers. The first transatlantic slave trades did not occur until the early 1500s, when the Portuguese slavers brought Africans to Hispaniola. By the 1600s, the slave trade to the Americas was booming. Local slave labor (Indians) proved insufficient for the large plantations being established on various Caribbean islands and in South America.

The slave trade was not a haphazard undertaking. A process had developed over the years that allowed the business—the purchase, collection, transportation, and sale of slaves—to run like clockwork. In the early years of the trade the Europeans would actively raid African villages for captives. Later they established alliances with African heads of state and merchants to supply them with marketable "goods." The traders had the Asante and Dahomey kingdoms (present-day Ghana and Benin, respectively) to thank for their success in acquiring slaves. Some scholars say these countries, in particular, acted as clearinghouses or middlemen for the traders from the late 1600s to the 1800s.

Perhaps bound for market, a woman in the Caribbean balances a tray of fruit on her head. The women of the African diaspora stayed true to their native cultures both wittingly and unwittingly, from the languages they spoke to the deities they worshiped to the ways in which they performed their labors.

Preceding pages: Framed in the peephole of a mud wall, a woman carries a pail of water in the village of Sangha, Mali. Only a few centuries ago, villagers like her across West Africa faced the grim prospect, on any given day, of being kidnapped and sold into slavery.

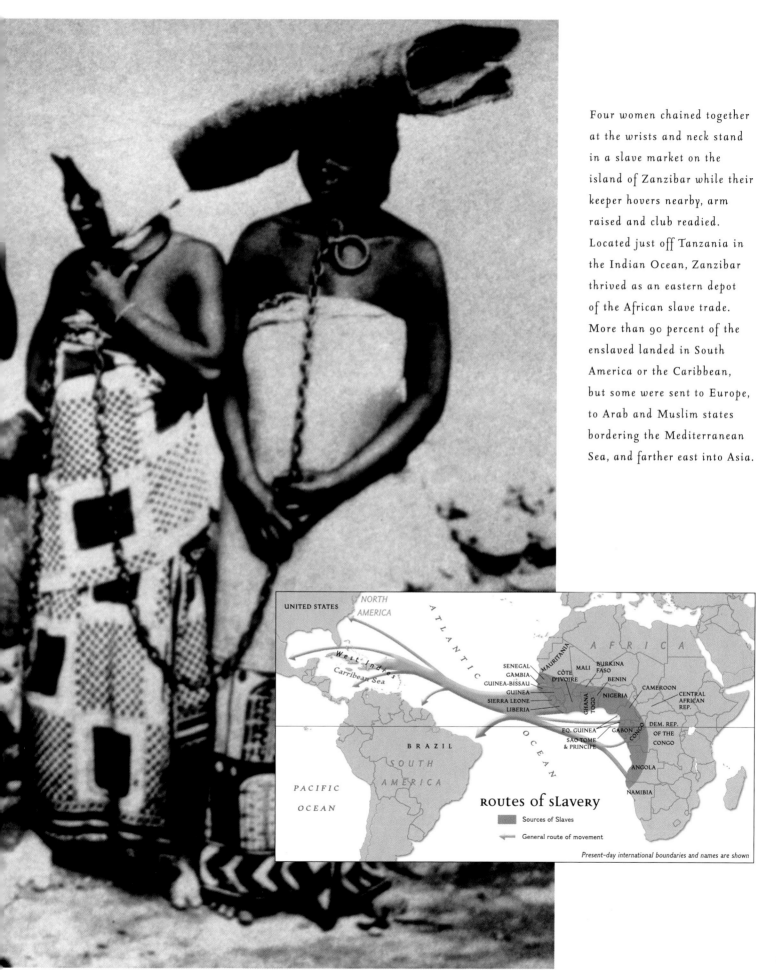

Four women chained together at the wrists and neck stand in a slave market on the island of Zanzibar while their keeper hovers nearby, arm raised and club readied. Located just off Tanzania in the Indian Ocean, Zanzibar thrived as an eastern depot of the African slave trade. More than 90 percent of the enslaved landed in South America or the Caribbean, but some were sent to Europe, to Arab and Muslim states bordering the Mediterranean Sea, and farther east into Asia.

routes of sLavery

Sources of Slaves

General route of movement

Present-day international boundaries and names are shown

The slave traders stopped at coastal markets where sellers—sometimes Africans— would bring their "merchandise." Some individuals were kidnapped and sold to the slavers. Some were sold by their own people in times of economic and environmental hardship. The majority of the individuals, however, were prisoners captured in war. (Sometimes the warring parties enslaved the prisoners themselves, but slavery in the homelands was very different from slavery in the New World.) The captives frequently had to walk long distances from the interior to the coast; it is estimated that 5 to 10 percent of the people destined for the slave trade died before they even were sold to the Europeans. The sellers bartered the human lives for textiles, guns and ammunition, knives, ironware, beads, and other goods. In 1714, records show that a young woman from the Asante region was sold for two small lengths of blue woolen cloth, seven guns, and 22 sheets. Their transactions complete, the traders sailed to the next market. Eventually, the traders dropped their cargo at large trading forts—the largest called castles—to await the transatlantic voyage.

Trading forts lined the western coast of Africa from Senegal down to Angola. (There were also some along Madagascar and southeastern Africa.) Built at various times throughout the slave trade era by the Dutch, Portuguese, French, British, and other Europeans, the majority of the forts were in place by 1740. They were powerful symbols of a world hungry for profit at the expense of humanity. Some of these castles were destroyed, but others—Gorée Island, Cape Coast Castle, Elmina Castle—still stand witness to the horrors committed against the people of Africa.

Just off the shores of Dakar, Senegal, stands one of the most important trading forts: Gorée Island. Over the course of three centuries, this tiny island temporarily housed millions of people. At any one time, thousands of men and women were crammed into the fort's tight quarters. Even today there is a pervasive spirit of the human cargo that was captured and stored there, awaiting a slave ship's arrival. Anna Marie Falconbridge, wife of Alexander Falconbridge, a doctor and commercial agent, wrote in 1791 of the horrors she witnessed at Bance Island—a small trading fort near Freetown, Sierra Leone: "Involuntarily I strolled to one of the windows a little before dinner, without the smallest suspicion of what I was to see—judge then what my astonishment and feelings were, at the sight of between two and three hundred victims, chained and parcelled out in circles, just satisfying the cravings of nature from a trough of rice placed in the center of each circle." Falconbridge would never forget the haunting eyes and the unimaginable story they told. The conditions at Bance Island were typical of those at most trading forts found along the West African coast.

A Black Madonna and Child presented to King Louis XI of France in the 15th century became the subject of this painting 300 years later. European art is rich with similar images that predate the first appearance of African slaves on the continent by many centuries. Apparently legends of ancient Black goddesses and queens, such as the Queen of Sheba, inspired the creation of this mysterious Christian icon. While beauty and divinity were ascribed to the Black Madonna, Black women kept as slaves in Europe were categorically debased.

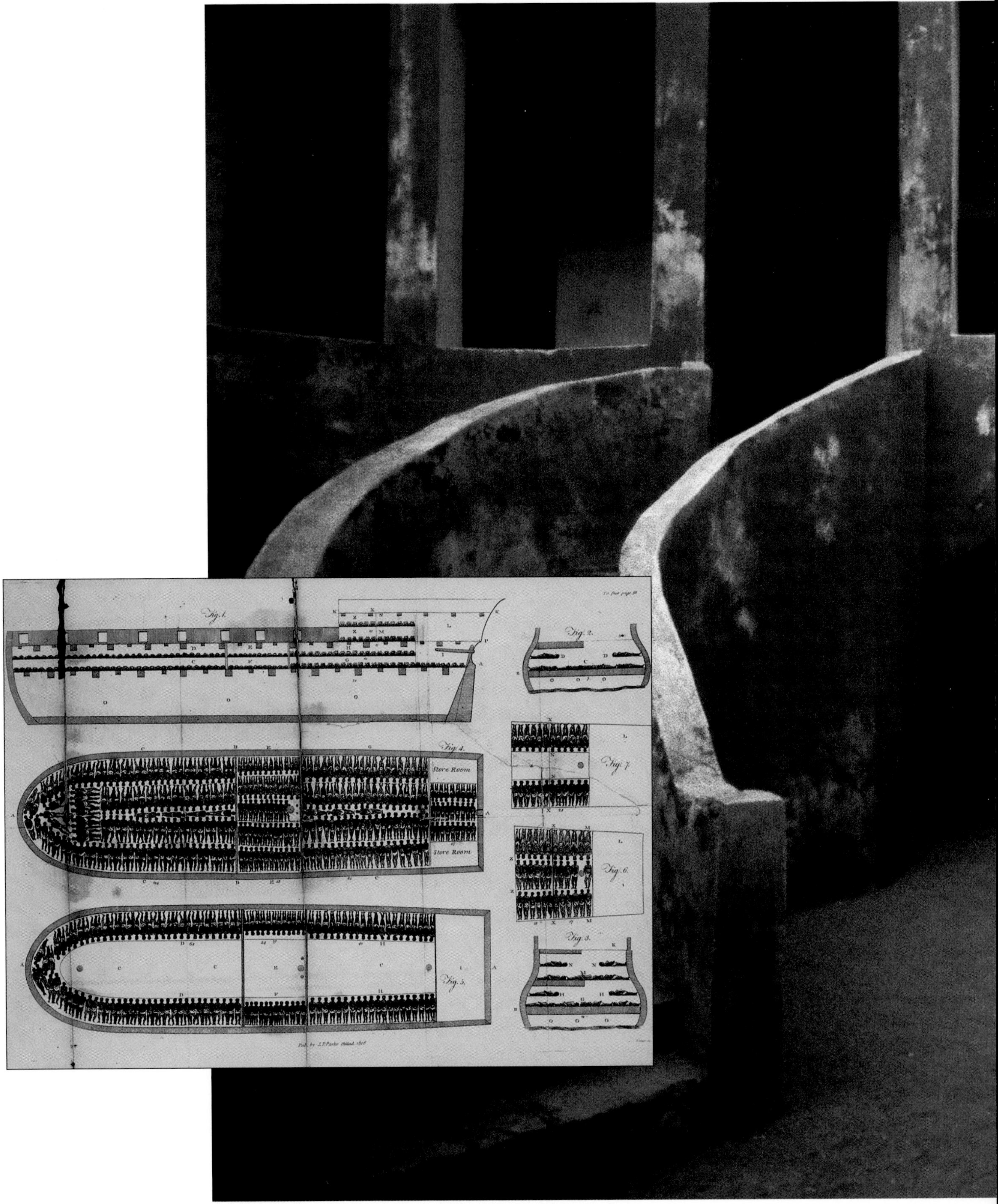
Fig. 1.
Fig. 2.
Fig. 3.
Fig. 4.
Store Room
Store Room
Fig. 5.
Fig. 6.
Fig. 7.

Many captives in Africa's slave trade began their torturous enslavement in European-built fortresses along Africa's west coast. Traditionally called castles but better understood as dungeons, these were holding places designed to break the human spirit. Those who survived the castles were herded through so-called "doors of no return"—of which the most infamous is this one found on Gorée Island—onto waiting ships. A cross section (left) of the Brookes, a British slaver, shows 482 African men, women, and children packed belowdecks for the journey through the Middle Passage.

Once at the fort, the slavers attempted to break the captives down spiritually and mentally to prepare them for their voyage of no return. The slavers separated the men from the women and children; they overcrowded them into small rooms; they let them out only once a day to relieve themselves; they shackled their necks and feet to a 22-pound iron ball; they fed them only once a day; they flogged and beat them at their pleasure; they had sentries standing guard to shoot anyone who attempted to escape. Women often suffered the additional terror of rape. Scholars estimate that 10 to 20 percent of the captives perished at the forts due to disease, diarrhea, and infected wounds caused by torture, branding, and maltreatment. The nightmare of the slaves' existence at Bance, Gorée, and other forts would only escalate once they boarded the slave ships.

The majority of the ships or frigates used to cross the Atlantic were not specifically built to carry human cargo. Some of the boats involved, like the *Amistad*, were small and fit only for commodities such as gold, ivory, and rice. This did not hinder the slavers. They placed wooden platforms between the decks to create additional space to house the captives. These confined areas were often only four to five feet high; one reportedly was only 14 inches high. The traders shipped the slaves in either a "loose pack" or "tight pack"— fewer slaves or more slaves—depending on a slaver's level of greed and humanity. The early years of the trade saw many merchants tight-packing the slaves, believing it reaped a maximum profit for the trip; however, in the 17th and early 18th centuries, the mortality rate hovered around 25 percent for the transatlantic passage. Unsanitary conditions, overcrowding, inadequate ventilation, and dehydration all contributed to the high rate of death. The rate dropped to 15 percent after 1730, and down to between 5 and 10 percent by the 19th century, after the slavers realized there was a direct correlation between better shipboard conditions and a healthy cargo.

Regardless, conditions for the slaves aboard ship were deplorable. The men were shackled and chained together in pairs, while the women and children were unfettered in a separate hold. The slave merchants kept the women they deemed comely near the doorway of the ship's hold to gratify their sexual demands. Dr. Alexander Falconbridge wrote in his 1788 *Account of the Slave Trade on the Coast of Africa* that "The officers are permitted to indulge their passions among them at pleasure and sometimes are guilty of such excesses as disgrace human nature." Many of the captives, male and female, were whipped and otherwise tortured.

Some slaves refused to take such treatment without a fight. Historians have proof of more than 200 shipboard revolts. Unfortunately, close to 99 percent ultimately ended in failure. One infamous revolt occurred on the French ship *Sultane*. Bound for the New World, the ship left Gorée Island in November 1750, carrying slaves who previously were involved in an uprising against European dealers. A few days out of port, the Africans attacked their captors, killing one-third of the crew. Eventually the Africans were subdued, but not until 230 of them had been killed. Another incident involved the British slave ship *Thomas*. In September 1797, it sailed for the Americas. Not long into the journey, two women, who were given leave to roam freely, found and distributed weapons to their fellow captives. A fighting force of more than 200 men managed to escape their holds and slaughter the crew; they kept two crew members alive to steer the ship back to Africa. The slaves' success was short-lived, though. A British frigate encountered the commandeered *Thomas* and managed to retake it. The ship turned around; the Africans were taken to Saint Domingue (Haiti) in the Caribbean.

Over the course of the transatlantic slave trade, the Caribbean received more than 50 percent of the slaves—spread out over numerous European colonies. Caribbean ports of call included Aruba, St. Martin, Mexico, Cuba, Hispaniola, Jamaica, Puerto Rico, Trinidad, Barbados, the British Virgin Islands, Grenada, Guadeloupe, Martinique, Dominica, and Saint Lucia. South America's Brazil received the single largest share of the trade: 38 percent. The North American colonies received roughly 5 percent. The New World colonies were lands of untold wealth and hope for many colonists, but just the opposite for the slaves.

Upon arriving in the New World colonies, the human cargo disembarked from the filthy bowels of the ships. The Africans reeked of the stench of hundreds of men, women, and children who had lived and died at sea. One by one, they were splashed with buckets of salty seawater—a bid to wash away the weeks and months of inhumane degradation they had endured. They moved away from the ship, in chains, marching toward the slave auction and a life of servitude.

Throughout the 300-plus years of overt slave trade, the total number of Africans who survived the transatlantic crossing—the Middle Passage—is estimated at 12 to 15 million. The majority of those transported were men. Most African societies placed a higher value on women—they performed much of the hard labor and also were needed for reproductive purposes—and so the women were not sold as often to the slave traders. It is estimated that young girls and women (age 14 to 30) made up only 25 percent of the slaves imported to the New World. But many of these women were survivors, and they left a lasting legacy.

In the 1800s, a beautiful young Angolan woman named Anastácia arrived at the port of Bahia (Salvador) on a slave ship via the infamous Portuguese slave fort on São Tomé. She was perhaps 15 years old. Lord Abaete, a wealthy sugar plantation owner, purchased her to work as domestic help in his household in Rio; Anastácia would be required to serve him in all capacities, including to bear him children. (Colonists in Brazil and other South American countries commonly recognized their children born to slaves; the children were considered freeborn.) Anastácia boarded in the main house and was frequently forced to submit to her master. Before long, Anastácia was giving birth to child after child, each dying as unceremoniously as it had lived. Since Anastácia proved unable to give birth to healthy children, Lord Abaete reduced her from house servant to field hand. She was sent to his plantation located in the interior of Bahia state.

On the plantation she discovered that in the countryside, far removed from the strict Catholic mores of town society, the traditional African religions were flourishing. In an effort to maintain order and obedience, the masters were more lenient and tolerant of the slaves' beliefs and rituals. The majority of the slaves in the state of Bahia were of

Yoruban descent—from the area of present-day Nigeria and Benin—so the Yoruba religion, which worshiped one supreme being and several lesser deities, predominated. Anastácia found comfort in the ancient beliefs and soon became a follower of the religion.

One night, it is said, Anastácia went into a trance and Yemanjá, goddess of the sea and the mother of all gods, spoke to the people through her. Yemanjá implored that "All those who have good legs should run away in order to set up a land of welcome for the gods of Africa. And the others, those who cannot shake the weight of their chains, those who are too young or too old, or too broken, they should from now on be able to look at the masters in the eyes, right in the eyes."

News of Yemanjá's pronouncement through Anastácia spread quickly from plantation to plantation. From that moment on, the African people of Bahia hung on Anastácia's every word. This caused a commotion among the slave owners. They demanded that Anastácia's owner quiet her so she would stop sowing mutinous ideas. He shackled Anastácia with a metal neck collar and made her wear a metal face mask with a mouth

European slave traders often paid for their human cargo in manillas, open bracelets cast from copper, brass, or iron. African dealers also accepted gold, silver, tobacco, livestock, iron, guns, gunpowder, textiles, glass, cowrie shells, and more. By 1700, rum had become—and remained—the preferred form of payment.

Opposite: A contemporary Surinamese woman wears a kottomisie, an oversize outfit designed to conceal the female figure. Outraged wives of colonial Dutch planters insisted that Black slave women dress in this manner to deflect the white men's advances.

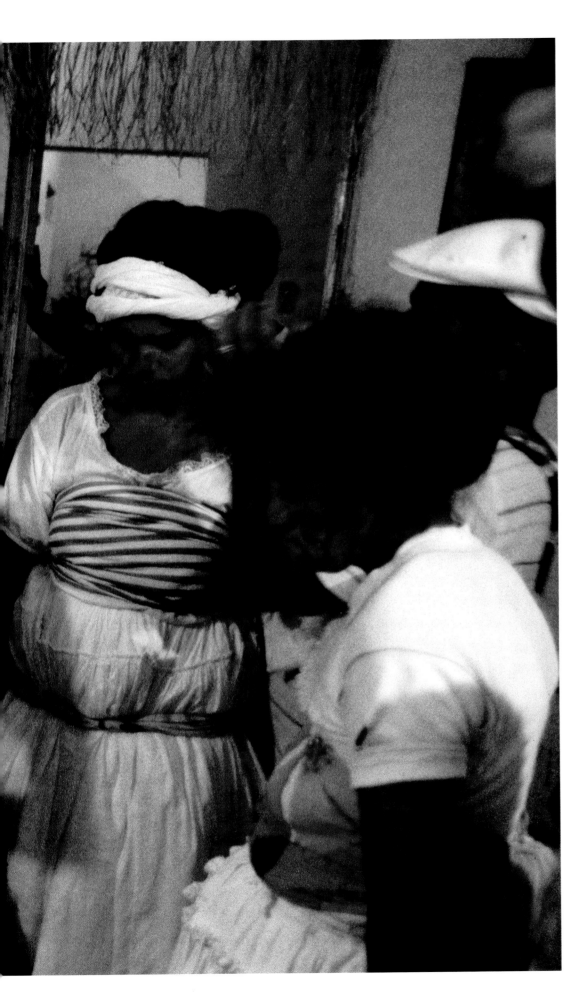

Young women dress in preparation for a Candomblé ceremony in Salvador, Brazil. An Afro-Brazilian religion, Candomblé blends elements of Catholicism with traditional religious beliefs and practices that were brought over by West African Yoruban slaves. Worshiping powerful female ancestors and goddesses, such as the one depicted by the wood carving above, remains central to Yoruban religious custom today.

clamp and snout that had very small breathing holes. He hoped this would stop Anastá-cia, but it did not. She used her beautiful, piercing blue eyes to communicate Yemanjá's message, imparting self-confidence and strength to her fellow slaves. Legend says she could stare into a person's very soul. In essence, her very presence was incentive enough to foment rebellion among the slaves.

Realizing Anastácia could still incite the slaves to revolt, Lord Abaete sold her to a slave dealer, who tried unsuccessfully to sell her on the open market. No slave owner dared risk having her around his slaves. The slave dealer threw Anastácia into a dungeon so no other slaves could see her and fall under her command. But the dungeon walls could not stop Anastácia's influence, so the dealer moved her to a deeper dungeon, hoping that the depth would quell her power. She was found dead some days later in her cell, the collar and mouth clamp cutting deeply into her throat. Word traveled swiftly through the slave grapevine; Anastácia quickly became a martyr and was worshiped by all who believed in her and in her message.

Her unselfishness, strength, and bravery in the face of her oppressors still inspires thousands of faithful practitioners of Candomblé—a religion that fuses Yoruban beliefs and Catholicism—in Bahia today. Though not officially beatified, Anastácia is revered as a saint, especially by women, who value her spirituality and self-confidence. Her legend perhaps inspires more than she herself did when she was alive.

In a similar fashion, Nanny, Queen of the Maroons, inspired slaves on the island of Jamaica. They drew courage and strength from her presence and continued to long for her after her death. Even today her legend and spirit are a tangible part of Jamaican culture. There are many tales about Nanny; some have their origins in partial truths, while many more are rooted in conjecture and folklore.

It is believed that Nanny arrived in Jamaica in the late 1600s. She was from the Asante Kingdom in West Africa. As she was led off the slave ship, she escaped her captors and headed for the hills, or mountains in this case—the Blue Mountains. Nanny never knew a day of slavery. She joined the Windward Maroons—one of several bands of slaves and indentured servants who had been abandoned by their Spanish masters when the British took over the island in 1655, and who refused to return to slavery. (Maroon comes from the Spanish cimarrón for "wild" or "fugitive.") Nanny eventually became the Windward Maroons' political and spiritual chief, leading them in many battles against the British in the First Maroon War (1720–1739), trying to claim peace and freedom for her people.

Nanny, Queen of the Maroons and a symbol of freedom, graces Jamaica's $500 bill. This fiercely independent African woman fled captivity and became the leader of the Windward Maroons, a community of fugitive slaves living in Jamaica's eastern Blue Mountains. The Windward Maroons still govern themselves in Jamaica and host an annual festival to honor Nanny's memory.

Nanny was an obeah—a medicine woman—and many people believed she was blessed with supernatural powers. She knew both magic and herbal potions and never hesitated to use them, whether for healing or for fighting. A popular story has Nanny presiding over a boiling cauldron at the confluence of the Stony and Nanny Rivers. Legend has it that her enemies succumbed to the waters of the cauldron whenever they came to capture or conquer the Maroon people. They somehow fell in and disappeared. Nanny also used chants, dances, and herbal infusions to invest her warriors with superior strength. Nanny herself was indestructible. Bullets could not hurt her. One tale has her catching musket balls and spitting them back at the British, killing several men with one "shot."

Beyond all of the folklore, Nanny was undoubtedly a superior leader. She had a powerful fighting spirit that instilled courage, confidence, and loyalty in her followers. And although Nanny Town—the stronghold of the Windward Maroons, and now nothing more than an overgrown site of crumbled stone walls—fell to the British in 1734, Nanny kept organizing new offenses and leading her then-scattered Maroons into battle. Nanny wholeheartedly disagreed with the peace treaty signed in 1739 between the British and Cudjoe, leader of the Clarendon Maroons, on behalf of all Jamaica's Maroons. Under the agreement, the Maroons were granted their freedom in exchange for their assistance in quelling any future slave rebellions. Nanny found this morally reprehensible.

Nanny died around 1750. The story says she died not by the hands of any white man, but instead by those of a militia of black men, formed specifically to hunt her down. Nanny was buried on a hill in Moore Town, in the Asante tradition. Her memorial reads

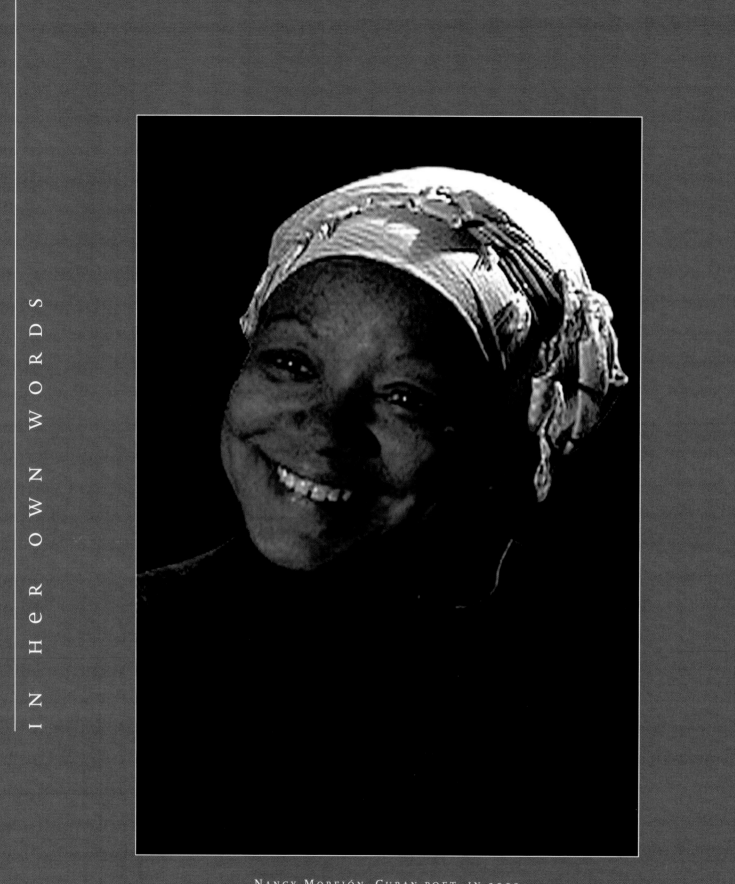

NANCY MOREJÓN, CUBAN POET, IN 2001

NANCY MOREJÓN

A native of Havana, Cuba, she is respected
internationally as a poet and anthologist.
Her works have been published in many languages.
This excerpt is from her poem "Black Woman."

I can still smell the spray of the sea they
   made me cross.
The night, I can't remember.
Not even the ocean itself could remember.
But I can't forget the first Alcatraz I saw.
High up, the clouds, like innocent
   witnessing presences.
By chance, I have forgotten neither my lost
   coast, nor my ancestral tongue.
They brought me here and here
   I have lived.
And because I worked like a beast
Here I was born again. How many a
   Mandinga legend have I resorted to.
I rebelled....

"Nanny of the Maroons. National Hero of Jamaica. Beneath this place known as Bump Grave lies the body of Nanny, indomitable and skileed." Nanny's legend remains a symbol of the desire never to yield to captivity, and it continues to inspire and unify the people of Jamaica. Today, she is revered and cherished as a national heroine; her likeness graces the Jamaican $500 bill. For many people, this validates the importance of Nanny.

Jamaica was not the only country in the West Indies where Africana women knew the cruelty of slavery and hungered for freedom. Bermuda, too, saw its share of unrest and rebellion, but none more remarkable than that of Mary Prince. Born at Brackish-Pond, Bermuda in 1788, Prince became the first African-British woman to escape slavery.

Prince's parents—her mother a domestic servant and her father a sawyer for a shipbuilder—belonged to two different masters and lived on separate plantations; Prince lived with her mother and was the property of Charles Myners. When Prince was very young, Myners died and she and her mother were sold to Captain Darrel. Darrel gave them to his daughter's family—the Williamses. He had bought Prince as a gift for his grandchild, Betsey, who was around the same age as Prince. Betsey treated Prince as a pet, and often led her around and referred to her as "my little nigger."

At the age of 12, Prince was hired out to Ms. Pruden, who lived in an adjoining parish in a large house by the sea. Anguished at leaving her mother, Miss Betsey, and Betsey's mother, Prince struggled to feel comfortable in her new surroundings and eventually discovered a small measure of happiness. Her stay was cut short, however, when Mrs. Williams died. Mr. Williams, who had grown impoverished, decided to sell Prince and her siblings. Mr. Williams forced Prince's mother to take Prince and her two sisters, Hannah and Dinah, to market at Hamble Town. Prince wrote in her memoirs:

> I, as the eldest, stood first, Hannah next to me, then Dinah; and our mother stood beside, crying over us. My heart throbbed with grief and terror so violently, that I pressed my hands quite tightly across my breast, but I could not keep it still, and it continued to leap as though it would burst out of my body.... At length the vendue master, who was to offer us for sale like sheep or cattle, arrived, and asked my mother which was the eldest. She said nothing, but pointed to me. He took me by the hand, and led me out into the middle of the street, and, turning me slowly round, exposed me to the view of those who attended the vendue. I was

A portrait of female strength and self-assuredness, the famed Rachel Pringle sits outside her hotel tavern in Bridgetown, Barbados. Daughter of a mixed marriage, Pringle was also a talented businesswoman whose late 18th-century establishment was known as a place to enjoy fine food and the company of fine women. The illustration shows a young Rachel in the background, flanked by her husband (right) and father.

A Frenchman traveling in Brazil in the 1830s sketched these 16 enslaved women, whose varied hairstyles, jewelry, patterns of ritual scarring, and even physical features suggest different African homelands. The finery of the clothing and accoutrements of these women calls into question the artist's motivation for making the drawing.

surrounded by strange men, who examined and handled me in the same manner that a butcher would a calf or a lamb he was about to purchase, and who talked about my shape and size in like words—as if I could no more understand their meaning than the dumb beasts.... I saw my sisters led forth, and sold to different owners; so that we had not the sad satisfaction of being partners in bondage.

Over the next several years, Prince had many different owners and performed a variety of labors—ranging from domestic servant to field hand to salt miner. Her owners beat and raped her; the chemicals at the salt plantation disfigured her arms and legs. In 1826, 38-year-old Prince married a free Black man; however, by West Indian law, she remained the property of her masters, the Woods.

Two years later, Prince accompanied the Woods to England and managed to escape; she sought refuge with the Moravian Church. She appealed to the British Anti-Slavery Society for financial and legal aid. Prince received enough money through donations to buy her freedom, but the Woods refused to allow the purchase. The Woods returned to Bermuda without Mary since the authorities could not force Prince to return to them. If Prince had returned to Bermuda she would likely have suffered the punishments meted out to runaway and problem slaves—beatings and most likely another sale. She chose to remain in England and never see her husband again, rather than to suffer the indignities of slavery one more day.

After the Woods left, Prince was nominally no one's slave, but legally she still belonged to the Woods. She wanted her freedom. She took her case to court and to the public. The vivid account of her life was published in London and in Edinburgh in 1831. The History of Mary Prince, a West Indian Slave, Related by Herself gave the world its first autobiographical account of the life of a slave woman. Instantly popular, the book garnered her a modicum of fame and may have influenced the English Parliament: England abolished slavery within its borders and its colonies in 1834. It is not known when Prince died, but her spirit and character live on in her narrative.

England soon knew another strong Black woman from the Caribbean: Mary Seacole, a woman who would earn the name "the Black Florence Nightingale." Born Mary Jane Grant in 1805 in Kingston, Jamaica, to a free Black woman and a Scottish Army officer, Seacole was part of a well-to-do family of mulattoes. As a Jamaican mulatto, she and approximately 35,000 other mulattoes were free, but they had very few other rights. They were not allowed to vote, hold public office, enter professions, or inherit much in the

This 1859 marble bust captures the compassion and strength of Mary Seacole. A self-educated nurse of great skill and resolve, she was lovingly called "Mother Seacole" by British soldiers in her care during the Crimean War. A London Times reporter observed at the time that "few names were more familiar to the public during the late Crimean war than that of Mrs. Seacole."

way of family fortunes. They were, however, usually very well educated since white planters held onto the custom of sending their Black children to schools in Europe.

The formal schooling, along with the informal education Seacole received from her mother, provided her with an extraordinary wealth of knowledge. Seacole's mother ran a profitable boardinghouse that catered to a British military clientele; she was also a medicine woman familiar with the treatment of tropical diseases, general ailments, and wounds. Her techniques, learned on plantations, were known as "Creole medical arts." They combined the inherited African knowledge of herbal medicine with the skills of midwifery. From her mother, Seacole inherited a "yearning for medical knowledge and practice."

Seacole excelled at doctoring, but she also relished adventure and travel. When she was a young woman, she took trips to England, the Bahamas, Haiti, and Cuba—at first with relatives, and later by herself. When she was in her 30s, she married Edward Horatio Seacole, who died shortly after their marriage. Her mother died around the same time. After mourning the deaths of her husband and mother, Seacole opened her own boardinghouse; many of her boarders were military surgeons who readily shared their knowledge with her when they learned of her aptitude for medical care. In 1850, Seacole journeyed to Cruces, New Grenada, to visit her brother. This move finally afforded Seacole the opportunity to live as a truly free woman. She reveled in her new life as an "unprotected female, full of confidence in my own powers."

For the next two to three years, Seacole moved around Central America and the Caribbean—Jamaica, Colombia, Panama—always setting up a hotel and administering to the sick and needy. She did not stay in one place for long; her wanderlust was too great. In nearly every location, Seacole tended to the victims of cholera outbreaks. She formulated new methods for the treatment of cholera and other tropical diseases, using her knowledge of traditional medicines and herbs. Her skills and nurturing nature endeared her to all who encountered her—be it as a patient or as a boarder in one of the many hotels she set up in each location.

In 1854, news of the war in the Crimea reached Seacole. She wrote: "No sooner had I heard of war somewhere, than I longed to witness it; and when I was told that many of the regiments I had known so well in Jamaica had left England for the scene of action, the desire to join them became stronger than ever." Seacole went to England to offer her services to the British Army, as a nurse for the wounded; however, racial discrimination thwarted her plans and she could not secure an official appointment. Undeterred, Seacole headed to the Crimea at her own expense.

Near Balaclava, in Turkey, she set up another boardinghouse—the British Hotel—to provide the servicemen with various amenities, including a small shop and a canteen; in addition, the hotel served as a hospital, where she nursed sick and dying British soldiers. She also volunteered her services at other military hospitals, treating the French, Turks, and British alike. Many people, believing war no place for a respectable woman, criticized Seacole for her actions. (Renowned British nurse Florence Nightingale, also in the Crimea, suffered the same criticisms; however, the two women never joined forces against their detractors. According to some records, Nightingale even refused to work with Seacole.)

Although Seacole had many critics, her hospitality and medical skills won over the soldiers. She became a revered and respected mother figure—one recognized in Europe as a healer who always took her bag into the thick of battle. An army surgeon at a Balaclava battlefield said that Seacole "was always equal to the occasion." From a medical standpoint, the herbal remedies and techniques Seacole used to treat wounds and infections were comparable to the successful treatments and methods used by doctors until the development of antibiotics revolutionized medicine in the mid-20th century.

For her valiant services in the Crimea, a grateful British nation fêted Seacole on her return after the war. In the years to come, Seacole was awarded the Crimean Medal, the French Legion of Honor, and a Turkish medal. Seacole wrote about her experiences in a striking 1857 autobiography entitled The Wonderful Adventures of Mrs. Seacole in Many Lands. The book was enormously popular at the time, chronicling how she never experienced slavery, how she was educated, and how she traveled in Central America and the Crimea.

Seacole spent her remaining years traveling between England and Jamaica. She died in 1881. As a nurse and healer, she demonstrated such skill and compassion that some argue that Florence Nightingale should be called the Anglo Mary Seacole. As a person, she led such a life of adventure and valor that she influenced people to rethink their prejudices. ♀

LOVE and BEAUTY --- SARTJEE the HOTTENTOT VENUS.

The drums of Africa
still beat in my heart.

—Mary McLeod Bethune

3 out of slavery

My grandmothers were strong.
They followed plows and bent to toil.
They moved through fields sowing seed.
They touched earth and grain grew.
They were full of sturdiness and singing.
My grandmothers were strong.

—from "Lineage,"
    by Margaret Walker Alexander

from the earliest days of the New World's colonization, European colonists practiced slavery. The institution of slavery grew from its strongholds in the Caribbean, South America, and Central America to an even greater strength in North America. The first Africans—numbering "20 and odd"—arrived in Jamestown, Virginia, in 1619 on a Dutch frigate, but the importation of slaves was minimal in the North American colonies until the 18th century. Only then did the institution of slavery grow and gain structure.

The diverse natures of the colonial powers in North America—French, British, Dutch, Spanish, to name but a few—resulted in differing ideological attitudes toward slavery. The South needed large numbers of workers to farm the labor-intensive crops grown on its plantations, whereas the trade- and industry-dependent North did not. The French and Spanish were more lenient, while the British were more rigid. Thus the manner in which slaves were treated depended largely on two factors: where they were living and who were their owners. The different slave practices only became more pronounced after the United States came into existence. The practice of buying people and using them in base ways was pervading life in the New World. But the dignity and traditions of Black peoples prevailed and revealed themselves in astonishing ways.

Jamaican lore embraces the belief that the revolutionary Nanny, Queen of the Maroons, used magic in the 1600s to defeat the British in the mountains of Jamaica. Similar notions exist about a young slave woman from Barbados in Salem, Massachusetts, in the late 1600s. Her supposed witchcraft touched off one of the most infamous events in

In an image widely circulated by women's antislavery associations on both sides of the Atlantic, a bound female slave implores her captor—or perhaps her deliverer—"Am I Not a Woman and a Sister?" While the slogan and image clearly link the two liberation movements, many abolitionists were sharply divided on the subject of women's rights.

Preceding pages: Although young cotton pickers were physically tied to the fields and experienced great suffering, their dignity often remained intact.

early U.S. history: the Salem Witch Trials of 1692. A woman of unknown consequence, Tituba was owned by Rev. Samuel Parris. Ingrained with the magic and lore of her Carib-Indian and African heritage, Tituba entertained the Parris children and their friends with stories from her homeland. To the deeply puritanical society of Salem, these stories appeared to contain elements of the supernatural; the stories aroused fear in those who heard the tales.

In January 1692, young Elizabeth Parris, her cousin Abigail Williams, and their friend Ann Putnam exhibited strange screaming, convulsive, and trancelike behavior—a condition that soon spread to several other Salem girls. Physicians, unable to determine any physical cause, decided the girls were acting under the influence of demonic spells. Pressed to reveal who had cast the spells on them, in late February, the girls named three women: Tituba, Sarah Good, and Sarah Osburn.

Both Sarahs professed their innocence and vehemently denied any involvement, but on March 1, Tituba, perhaps coerced by the whip, confessed to the deed: "The devil came to me and bid me serve him." She also turned accuser and testified that there was a conspiracy of witches at work in Salem. Tituba and her co-accused were sent to prison in Boston to await their fates. Throughout the spring and summer, more people were accused of witchcraft. A special court was convened to hear the cases.

Many townspeople signed documents proclaiming the innocence of the accused; others insisted the defendants had harmed them. Several people claimed to have been

This copper badge proved that the slave who wore it could be hired out by his owner. Charleston instituted a slave badge system in order to regulate the hiring of slaves for jobs that would otherwise go to White people.

Opposite: A page from an Eastville, Virginia, planter's property book overlays a photo of a slave. The likeness and written word both identify human chattel. Each entry lists a slave's number, name, birth date, skin color, height, and unique markings such as "small Black moles on chin."

visited by ghosts, definitely influencing a guilty ruling. The number of convictions grew. By October 8, some 20 men and women had been executed, including Sarah Good (Sarah Osburn died in jail awaiting the gallows). But criticism of the witch hunt was mounting. On October 29, Governor William Phips dissolved the court, ruling that spectral evidence of witchcraft was inadmissible. Shortly thereafter the furor died down and the hunt ended.

Tituba managed to escape the hangman's noose. Her measure of naiveté and the great deal of affection she showed for Elizabeth, Abigail, and Ann when she testified helped in small part, but the children were the most instrumental in saving Tituba's life. They testified that Tituba no longer hurt them after she had confessed. Regardless, Rev. Parris refused

231 Born January 22 1825 Matilda Bevans Light Chesnut 5 2 8/10 Round face and good expression of countenance. Small black mole on the chin.

232 Born August 12th 1813 Mary Guy Yellow 5 4 Several marks on the nose and face from the effects of small pox; two small moles on the left cheek.

233 Born March 4th 1817 Emeline Jacob Light Chesnut 5 4 1/2 Some very small moles on the right cheek — two small moles in the palm of the right hand. Scar about an inch long in the palm of the right hand.

234 Born January 31st 1841 Louisa Rozell Light Chesnut 5 1 1/2 High cheek bones, small scar on each cheek; small eyes and short teeth.

235 Born Jany. 22d A.D. 1829 Jacob Church Dark Chesnut 5 9 8/10 Scar on the upper part of the nose between the eyes; scar near the corner of the left eye.

to pay for Tituba's imprisonment fees, so she spent a total of 13 months in jail until an unknown family living outside Salem paid her jailtime dues and appropriated her as their slave. For Tituba, the end of the Salem Witch Trials meant freedom from death, but not from servitude.

By regaling the children with stories, Tituba had been carrying on the grand tradition of oral storytelling, just one of many traditions slave women brought with them from their homelands. One other tradition was to give their children African names. In the mid-1700s, a slave woman from Natchitoches, Louisiana, gave birth to a daughter and, following tradition, named her Coincoin—"second daughter"—even though, as the French 1724 Code Noir for Louisiana decreed, the child was baptized in the Catholic Church and given the Christian name Marie-Thérèse.

Coincoin was born in 1742 to a woman owned by Louis Juchereau de St. Denis, the newly appointed governor of Natchitoches. It is presumed that St. Denis was her father. When St. Denis died, his daughter, Marie de Nieges de Soto, inherited Coincoin. Coincoin worked as a house servant and was treated mercifully by de Soto. Coincoin grew into a beautiful woman possessed of inordinate poise and strength; she was also, according to family lore, a skilled healer. De Soto was indebted to Coincoin for saving her life: Coincoin carefully nursed the White woman when she had yellow fever.

In 1767, when Coincoin was 25 years old, Claude Metoyer, a well-to-do plantation owner, arrived in Natchitoches and, by all accounts, was instantly attracted to the lovely mulatto woman. He arranged to lease Coincoin as his housekeeper. (It was a common practice for owners in the Southern states to "rent out" their slaves.) Coincoin moved into Metoyer's household with her four young children, becoming Metoyer's mistress in addition to his housekeeper. Over the years, Coincoin bore Metoyer several children. Outraged by Metoyer's concubinage, the local religious leaders pressed Metoyer to stop living in sin. Metoyer refused. In 1778, Metoyer purchased Coincoin and their youngest child from de Soto and quietly freed them. (By law, and this was true throughout the North American colonies, any child born to a slave woman was automatically a slave, and the property of the mother's owner.)

While it may never be known how Metoyer and Coincoin felt about each other, it is clear from their actions that the arrangement was satisfactory to both of them. After gaining her freedom, Coincoin remained with Metoyer for eight more years and bore him three more children (in total she bore Metoyer ten children). Coincoin at last left Metoyer's house in 1786 when he took a wife who could bear him a legitimate heir, as the Code Noir forbid interracial marriage. Metoyer obviously still cared for Coincoin, though: He deeded her 68 acres of land along the nearby Red River and a yearly annuity of $120.

Coincoin, then in her mid-40s, moved into a small cottage on the land with some of her children, and planted tobacco. Over the next ten years, with her annuity and the money she earned selling tobacco, Coincoin bought two of her non-Metoyer children; she also arranged with Metoyer to purchase from him over time the rest of their children in return for giving up the annuity. By 1793, Coincoin had enough money to attain an additional 500 acres of land from the Spanish territorial government. She used the land to graze livestock. Coincoin's success as a landowner kept growing. When she died in 1816 at the age of 74, she and her children had amassed more than 2,000 acres of land and more than 100 slaves. Coincoin's successful rise from slave to landowner can never be diminished.

Coincoin was not the only slave woman to take advantage of her circumstances to better her lot in life. The practice of powerful White slave-owning men having relationships with Africana women was not confined to Louisiana. It occurred wherever Black women found themselves, whether in Africa, the Caribbean, or the Americas. Perhaps one of the more well-known affairs was between President Thomas Jefferson and his slave Sally Hemings. Hemings's life as a mistress was quite different from that of Coincoin's but she also benefitted from her situation.

Hemings, whose given name is believed to have been Sarah, was a mulatto born in 1773 to Elizabeth "Betty" Hemings and her master, John Wayles, a British lawyer and slave-trading sea captain. Wayles was the father of Martha Wayles Jefferson, President Jefferson's wife. When Wayles died, Martha inherited the Hemings family, including three-year-old Sally. Sally Hemings spent her early years at Monticello, the Jefferson estate, running errands for Martha, her half-sister. Martha had a tiny silver bell she used to call Hemings and other slaves to her. Ironically, Hemings would later come to own the bell as a keepsake from Martha.

Provoked to action in 1781 by an abusive mistress, Elizabeth Mumbet Freeman (portrayed 30 years later) sued for her freedom in a Massachusetts courtroom and won. When asked how an illiterate slave woman learned about the "rights of man" upon which she based her legal argument, Freeman replied "by keepin' still and mindin' things."

Opposite: The frontispiece to Phyllis Wheatley's 1773 book of verse shows her with pen in hand. The slave was a gifted poet and the first Black writer to be published in America. Many White people found it hard to believe that a Black person was capable of such noble and artistic expression.

In this 1836 cartoon, future U.S. Vice President Richard M. Johnson reacts with dismay to newspaper attacks on his Black common-law wife, while political supporters and his mulatto daughters offer comfort. Johnson openly acknowledged his biracial offspring at a time when White men commonly disavowed the children that they fathered by Black women. Yet Johnson was hardly a champion of progressive race relations. When the mother of his daughters died, he took another slave woman as his common-law wife. When she ran away, he found her, sold her at a slave auction, and took her sister as his mistress.

When the Jeffersons' third daughter, Mary, was born in 1778, Hemings had the added duties of caring for her. Martha Jefferson gave birth to Lucy Elizabeth in May 1782; she never regained her strength and died a few months later. At this time, Jefferson swore he would never let affairs of state interfere with his devotion to his family. In July 1784, Jefferson went to Paris as the U.S. ambassador to France; he took his eldest daughter, Martha, with him. In 1787, he sent for his daughter Mary. That summer, 14-year-old Hemings and 8-year-old Mary traveled from the U.S. to London, where John and Abigail Adams received them. Mrs. Adams commented that Hemings was "quite a child" who "seems fond of [Mary] and appears good natured." Hemings was also blossoming into a beautiful young woman. According to the slave known as Isaac Jefferson, she was "mighty near white … very handsome, long straight hair down her back." Jefferson's grandson, Thomas Jefferson Randolph, later described her as "light colored and decidedly good looking." Following their two-week stay in London, Jefferson's French butler, Adrien Petit, escorted the two girls to Paris.

While in Paris, Hemings lived at one of three locations: Jefferson's residence, the Hotel de Langeac, or the Abbaye de Panthemont, where Martha and Mary Jefferson attended boarding school. While it is not known exactly where Hemings stayed, it is clear that she was trained in needlework and in the care of clothing so she could properly fulfill her role as lady's maid. Documents show that Hemings was occasionally paid a monthly wage the equivalent of two dollars. It is presumed that the affair between Jefferson and Hemings began in Paris in 1788.

By 1789, when Martha was introduced into proper French society, increased expenditures for clothing reflect that both she and Hemings wore attire befitting debutante and personal attendant. When the family returned to Virginia later that year, Hemings continued to perform the duties of household servant and lady's maid. Hemings's son Madison would later recall in an 1873 article, which appeared in the *Pike County Republican*, that Sally took "care of [Jefferson's] chamber and wardrobe." It is not known if Hemings remained in the Jefferson house or moved to the stone workmen's house called Weaver's Cottage, or to one of the new log cabins farther down Mulberry Row. At some point after 1792, according to Thomas Jefferson Randolph, she lived in one of the "servant's rooms" under the south terrace. From 1790 to 1808, she bore seven sons and daughters, all presumably fathered by Jefferson—they were all light-skinned, had reddish hair, and had many physical traits that resembled Jefferson's.

Jefferson never officially freed Hemings—though he did free five members of her family. When Jefferson died on July 4, 1826, his granddaughter Ellen Randolph Coolidge inherited Hemings. She likely gave Hemings "her time," a form of unofficial freedom that would allow Hemings to remain in Virginia, as the laws at the time required freed slaves to leave the state within a year. Hemings reportedly lived and died in Charlottesville, in the household of her sons, Madison and Eston. In 1998, DNA evidence proved that Jefferson most likely sired one, if not more, of Hemings's children.

a t the time of her death in 1835, Sally Hemings was one of 2.3 million Black people who populated the United States. Of this number, nearly one million were enslaved Black women in the southern states; the majority had been born slaves and never knew a day's freedom. But some refused to accept slavery as their lot in life. They desired freedom, and would do whatever was necessary to achieve it. In 1848, one young couple from Georgia pulled off what is considered the most daring slave escape in U. S. history: Light-skinned Ellen Craft and her husband, William, crossed the Mason-Dixon line posing as an elderly White male traveler and his Black male valet.

Ellen, a quadroon (one quarter Black), was born in Clinton, Georgia, in 1826 to a slave woman named Marie, a house servant. Her father, Maj. James Smith, was a cotton planter and slaveholder. He gave Ellen to his daughter, Eliza, as a wedding gift because it upset his wife that Ellen was always mistaken for one of her children. In 1837, Ellen moved to Macon with her new owner. There she soon encountered William Craft, a slave apprenticed to a cabinetmaker. Because William knew a trade, he was a highly valued slave and treated with more respect than usual. He was allowed his own clothes and dwelling—an arrangement that afforded him some degree of freedom and self-sufficiency.

Ellen and William longed for freedom and a life together. Initially, Ellen did not wish to marry and bear children into slavery; the two resolved to find a way to escape before they married. Yet as time wore on, they were "reluctantly driven to the sad conclusion, that it was almost impossible to escape from slavery in Georgia, and travel 1,000 miles across the slave States." They married in 1846, but they never stopped thinking about freedom. In December 1848, William had an audacious plan: They should pose as a White male slave owner and his slave and travel on public transportation, in full view of everyone, to the North. According to William, Ellen said "I think it is almost too much for us to undertake; however, I feel that God is on our side, and with his assistance, notwithstanding all the difficulties, we shall be able to succeed."

On December 21, Ellen boarded a northbound train posing as a sickly White

Thomas Jefferson's wife, Martha, gave this bell as a keepsake to her slave Sally Hemings, who was also her half-sister. It is one of the odd and obscure links between the reportedly tall, beautiful, fair-skinned Hemings and the Jefferson family. In 1802, a political enemy of Jefferson's insinuated the most intimate of relationships between the then-President of the United States and Hemings. Although some people still debate the issue, DNA evidence has shown that a Jefferson—it could have been Thomas's brother—fathered at least one child by Hemings.

gentleman suffering from acute rheumatism. She wore a poultice about her face and neck to hide her skin's smoothness; green-colored spectacles hid her fine eyes; to hide her illiteracy, she kept her right arm in a sling to avoid signing her name if the occasion arose; a top hat and cane completed her outfit. William settled into the section of the train reserved for coloreds. Using this subterfuge, Ellen and William made their way from Macon to Philadelphia. They traveled by train, steamer, and mail coach. Ellen was required to stay in character for five days, oftentimes deflecting questions about her too-civil treatment of her attendant slave and her judgment in taking a slave to Philadelphia, where abolitionists could help him escape.

After a number of close calls—including being questioned by train officials in Baltimore for the proof of slave ownership, which the train company required of anyone bringing slaves into Philadelphia—the Crafts arrived in Philadelphia on Christmas Day. They made their way to an abolitionist-run boardinghouse—a sympathetic passenger aboard the train had recommended it to William in case he wished to escape his master. There they were directed to free Black abolitionists William Still and Robert Purvis, who were amazed by the Crafts' daring. They arranged for the Crafts to stay with a Quaker family just outside Philadelphia, but soon it was felt that Philadelphia was too close to the South for the Crafts' safety, since word was spreading of their feat. The Crafts moved to Boston via the Underground Railroad, a secret network of people, places, and transportation that helped runaway slaves to freedom. Very little is known about the intricate details of the railroad because of the intense secrecy needed to make it work. Only a few memoirs—from conductors and conductees alike—serve to illustrate its proud history of numerous successes.

In Boston, William worked as a cabinetmaker and Ellen as a seamstress. They also learned to read and write. They became active in the antislavery movement, writing and making speeches, using their story for inspiration. In 1850, after word of how the Crafts had managed to escape reached the South, outraged slave owners pushed the Fugitive Slave Act through Congress. The act denied accused slaves the right to a trial and enacted stiff penalties for those individuals helping slaves escape. The Crafts' owners sent slave catchers after them; when that failed, they enlisted the help of President Fillmore, who mobilized an army of soldiers to find the Crafts. The Crafts became so sought-after that they couldn't risk sleeping in the same location twice. They were on the run again. The Vigilance Committee of Boston, a group of citizens who protected fugitive slaves from reenslavement, helped the Crafts reach Halifax, Nova Scotia, in Canada, where the couple boarded a ship bound for Liverpool, England. After arriving safely in England, the Crafts were at last free.

The American Anti-Slavery Almanac for 1840 ironically illustrates the very real physical tortures that slaves endured. "I give up for dead, and she wouldn't stop," recalled one former slave describing a brutal whipping by her mistress. "I said 'Old Mis', if I were you and you were me, I wouldn't beat you this way.'" Few White people empathized, viewing the abuse as discipline.

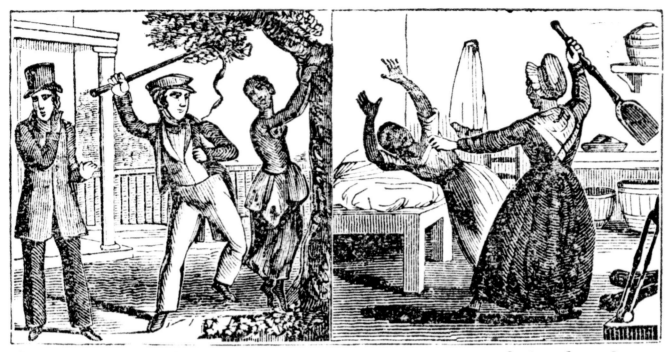

Showing how slavery improves the condition of the female sex.

In England, Ellen continued her profession as a seamstress while William returned to cabinetry. William published the story of his and Ellen's daring escape in 1860; *Running a Thousand Miles for Freedom* was received in London to popular acclaim. They lived in England for 19 years before returning to America in 1869.

Ellen and William Craft were successful in their bid for freedom. However, for every plot like theirs that succeeded, there were many more that did not. Earlier that same year, two teenage sisters from Washington, D.C., failed in their attempt to escape. Washington was the federal capital; it had a more transient—and foreign—population, and as such, it was more tolerant toward Black people. In the mid-1800s, Washington had a thriving free Black community—indeed there were more free Black people in the city than slaves. At the time, Georgetown and Foggy Bottom were, in fact, heavily populated sections of Washington that offered Black people a substantial residential, religious, and commercial existence. Most slaves in Washington worked as domestic servants, chauffeurs, and cooks. The consensus on the part of White people was that Washington, D.C. offered everything that a slave could want. But freedom was sweeter.

Paul and Amelia Edmonson were well known in the free Black Washington community. Paul was a free man, but Amelia was enslaved. All 14 of their children, by law, were born slaves. A few of them later managed to buy their freedom; however, most were hired out as servants. Emily and Mary (13 and 15 years old, respectively), exposed

A mid-19th-century painting entitled "On to Liberty" shows fugitive slaves arriving at a Union Army camp at daybreak after traveling under cover of darkness on the Underground Railroad. The railroad, an extensive, secret network of people and places that helped slaves escape the South, was also known to Black people as the "freedom train." Many slave spirituals mention the freedom train, and White people mistakenly assumed for years that slaves were referring to dying and going to heaven. In fact, the freedom train was very real. Along the tracks of the Underground Railroad, sympathetic White and Black people provided safe houses and other forms of aid, but the conductors, who risked everything to lead fugitives to freedom, were usually Black.

SOJOURNER TRUTH, ABOLITIONIST AND FEMINIST (1797-1883)

SOJOURNER TRUTH

Legendary for linking abolition and women's
rights in the 19th century, Truth gave her famous
"A'n't I a Woman" speech at a women's rights
gathering in 1851 in Ohio.

Nobody eber helps me into carriages or
ober mud puddles...! And a'n't I a woman?
Look at my arm! I have ploughed, planted,
and gathered into barns, and no man
could head me! And a'n't I a woman?
I could work as much and eat as much as
a man...and bear de lash as well! And
a'n't I a woman?...Den dat little man in
black dar, he say women can't have as
much rights as men, 'cause Christ wan't a
woman! Whar did your Christ come from?
From God and a woman! If de fust woman
God ever made was strong enough to
turn de world upside down all alone,
dese women togedder ought to be able to
turn it back, and get it right side up again!

Harriet Tubman (above at far left), who earned the nickname "Moses," poses with some of the slaves she led safely out of the South. Tubman reportedly carried a gun, not to defend herself against would-be White captors but to compel Black runaways inclined to give up. "Live North or die here," she would tell them.

Opposite: The capture and return of escaped slaves such as this woman in 1863 promised tempting rewards. The map (inset) shows the main routes of the Underground Railroad out of the South.

through their parents and freed siblings to all the benefits the free Black community had to offer, wished for their own freedom.

On the night of April 15, they made their way to the 7th Street Wharf, where abolitionists had arranged passage for them and other slaves on the Pearl. The 54-ton bay schooner, captained by Dan Drayton, a White abolitionist, would take them to Philadelphia. Seventy-seven slaves boarded the ship before it sailed down the Potomac River that night. Their freedom was short-lived. Before long, several slave owners discovered their slaves missing. It soon dawned on them that a mass escape had occurred.

A hundred-man posse was formed and the hunt was on. After learning from an informant that the slaves had escaped by river, the slave owners pressed a steamboat into service to overtake and bring back the Pearl. The steamboat caught up with the schooner at Point Lookout, some 140 miles downriver, where it lay at anchor awaiting calmer weather. The slaves were returned to Washington, D.C., where a mob of White residents had banded together to riot and to make an example of the 77 slaves. As a result, most of the slave owners sold their slaves to traders from New Orleans, Louisiana. Mary and Emily were among those sent south.

$50.00 Reward!!

Ran away from the Yard Corner of Jackson & Broad Streets, Augusta Ga. — on the evening of Tuesday 7th April 1863 a Woman "Dolly", whose likeness is here seen. —

She is thirty years of age, light Complexion — hesitates somewhat when Spoken to, and is not a very healthy woman — but rather good looking, with a fine set of teeth. Never Changed her Owner and has been a house Servant always. —— It is thought she has been enticed off by some White Man, being ____ ____ ____ this City, and belonging to a ____ ____ ____ For further particula____ ____ Poullain Esqr Augusta Ga. —

Augusta Police

Louis Manigault

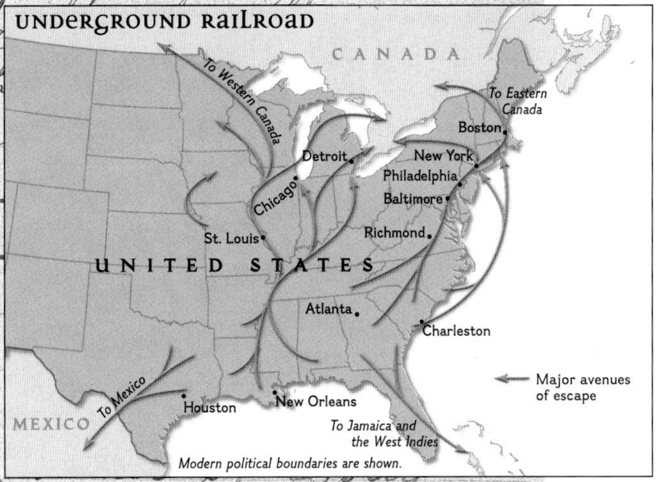

UNDERGROUND RAILROAD

CANADA

To Western Canada

To Eastern Canada

Boston

Detroit

New York

Philadelphia

Chicago

Baltimore

St. Louis

Richmond

UNITED STATES

Atlanta

Charleston

To Mexico

MEXICO

Houston

New Orleans

To Jamaica and the West Indies

← Major avenues of escape

Modern political boundaries are shown.

The Edmonsons approached various sympathetic organizations in Washington in an attempt to raise the funds necessary to buy back their daughters from the slave traders. Unsuccessful, they took their case farther afield. They appealed to the Anti-Slavery Society in New York, which directed them to Rev. Henry Ward Beecher. Moved by their pleas, Beecher and his church membership raised the $2,250 needed to purchase the girls' freedom and return them to their parents.

Beecher's congregation continued to provide for Mary and Emily, raising enough funds to send the girls to New York Central College in Cortland, New York, where the sisters worked as domestics to support themselves. In 1850 they attended a protest convention against the Fugitive Slave Act and met Frederick Douglass. In 1853, they both enrolled in Oberlin College in Ohio, but Mary, of frail health since the *Pearl* incident, died six months later of tuberculosis. Emily returned to Washington, D.C., and enrolled at Myrtilla Miner's Colored Girls School, a secondary education school. She later taught at the school, which would eventually be renamed the Miner Normal School and later become a part of Howard University. Emily remained friends with Douglass, who lived in nearby Anacostia, and continued her work in the abolition movement.

Mary and Emily's daring escape attempt and its aftermath inspired Harriet Beecher Stowe, Rev. Beecher's sister. She modeled characters and events in her seminal book, *Uncle Tom's Cabin*, after their story. The book—and by extension the Edmonson sisters—helped galvanize a nation at a time when public sentiment toward slavery was turning sour.

O n the heels of the 1850 Fugitive Slave Act, many Northern states passed personal liberty laws to protect runaway slaves and free Black people in their states. These actions served to antagonize the South, which saw the laws as an attack and affront to the Southern lifestyle, further fanning the flames for secession. With the advent of the Civil War, Northerners began to rectify the injustices they perceived. Education was seen as the means to human betterment. Following the Civil War, the Freedmen's Bureau, formed in 1865 to provide relief and services for Black people, established institutions of higher learning for newly freed slaves, Native Americans, and other non-Whites.

Susie Baker King Taylor did not attend one of these institutes of higher learning, but the education she managed to receive in the pre-Civil War years proved invaluable. Susie played an active and vital role in the Civil War. She was born into slavery in 1848 on the Isle of Wight, one of Georgia's Sea Islands and one of the many islands that are home

Diana Fletcher, a proud Black Indian woman of the mid-19th century, was the daughter of an African man who escaped slavery in Florida and a Seminole woman. Fletcher's mother died during the Indians' forced march by the U.S. government to Oklahoma in 1842. Her father remarried a Kiowa woman who raised Fletcher as her own. Many Indian villages, such as the Gingaskin Reservation in Northampton, Virginia, gave fugitive slaves refuge and allowed them to intermarry. Children from these unions were called Black Indians.

to the Gullah—Black people who retained much of the African culture and language that they brought with them, mostly from Sierra Leone, West Africa. She was a direct descendant of one of the first African slaves brought to the colony of Georgia in the early 1730s. When she was very young, she was sent to Savannah to live with her grandmother, a trusted slave who had been given leave to live on her own. She made a living bartering chickens and eggs for goods. Wanting Taylor to have a better life, Susie's grandmother arranged for a free Black woman to teach Taylor to read and write—even though it was illegal to educate slaves during the pre-Civil War years. This unusual upbringing would change Taylor's life.

When the Civil War began in 1861, Taylor and her grandmother moved with her uncle and his family to St. Simon's, one of South Carolina's Sea Islands. After the islands were liberated, the army recruited Taylor to teach the newly freed slaves to read. Shortly thereafter, Taylor left St. Simon's to care for her uncle and other relatives who had joined the Union's First South Carolina Volunteers. Only 14 years old, she first worked as a laundress, but because she could read and write, the Army pressed her into service as a nurse. She was the Army's first Black nurse; in the summer of 1863, she worked side by side with Clara Barton in Beaufort, South Carolina.

Taylor related her experiences in her 1902 autobiography, A Black Woman's Civil War Memoirs—the only memoirs of a Black woman's experiences in the Civil War. She was clearly proud of the duties she performed: "I was very happy to know my efforts were successful in camp, and also felt grateful for the appreciation of my service. I gave my services willingly for four years and three months without receiving a dollar. I was glad however, to be allowed to go with the regiment, to care for the sick and afflicted comrades." After the war, Taylor returned to teaching, but she never forgot the Black Civil War troops. Throughout her lifetime she supported them in their fight for equal pay and benefits.

Education summarily altered Susie Taylor's life. And education would bring another strong and independent woman to the Sea Islands during the Civil War. By the early 1860s, access to education (or even a small measure of literacy) was seen as critically important in making the move from enslavement to freedom. Young women such as Charlotte Forten Grimké undertook the serious matter of educating the Black women of the South.

Charlotte Forten Grimké was born in 1837 in Philadelphia, Pennsylvania, into a wealthy family of free Black abolitionists. Her grandfather, James Forten, Sr., was a successful sailmaker and advocate of abolition; his home was on occasion a way station on the Underground Railroad. Her grandmother and aunts were founding members of the Philadelphia Female Anti-Slavery Society, a biracial organization that took hold in 1833. Her parents, Mary and Robert Bridges Forten, were also active abolitionists.

When Grimké was quite young her mother died, and she was sent to live with her aunt who had married into the Purvis family, another prominent free Black abolitionist family. Because her father would not allow her to attend a segregated school, Grimké was privately tutored until her father sent her to the interracial Higginson Grammar School in Salem, Massachusetts. Grimké was the only non-White student in the school. She graduated with distinction and went on to higher education at Salem Normal School. Her achievements earned her a teaching position at the all-White Epes Grammar School. She was the first Black teacher in the Salem public school system.

While in Salem, Grimké followed in her family's abolitionist footsteps. She became an active member of the Female Anti-Slavery Society of Salem, an organization dedicated to providing aid to free Black people and to abolishing slavery. It was founded in 1832 by a group of free Black women. She frequently attended lectures where she heard, met, and was inspired by Ralph Waldo Emerson, Rev. Henry Ward Beecher, Senator Charles Sumner, Maria Weston Chapman, and many other famous antislavery activists.

In 1858, Grimké returned home to Philadelphia to recover from a recurring bout of tuberculosis. She had by now become a gifted writer and poet whose works appeared in numerous journals. Most contained strong antislavery themes. Her tragic story of young lovers, "Wind Among the Poplars," gained popularity largely because it illustrated the very human side of young Black people and their emotional situations.

During her convalescence, she applied for a teaching position in the south, still keen to continue spreading the abolitionist message. In 1862 she took up her new position on St. Helena Island, a South Carolina Sea Island. In late 1861, the plantation owners on these islands fled attack by the Union Navy, leaving behind some 10,000 slaves. The freedmen and -women proceeded to appropriate the lands for themselves. News of this liberation set off a wave of philanthropy in the North, as well as unscrupulous profiteering. The Pennsylvania Freedmen's Relief Association—a group of abolitionists, philanthropists, and Quakers who sought to educate and help ex-slaves—sent a small force of teachers south to educate the former slaves in what was called the Port Royal Experiment, a philanthropic and economic project that to some extent provided a blueprint for Reconstruction. Grimké was the first Black teacher to participate in the endeavor.

Grimké was excited by the prospect of teaching her fellow brothers and sisters who were newly freed. She later wrote of her first impressions of her new students in "Life

Susie Baker King Taylor, a nurse with the Union Army's First South Carolina Volunteers, is the only known Black woman to have written of her life during the Civil War. Her memoirs describe her experiences caring for the sick and dying during the "wonderful revolution," and her later life as a teacher, wife, and mother.

Following pages: Freed slaves take time away from the fields to care for their babies. This was a privilege rarely granted during slavery times, when Black mothers also feared being separated permanently from their children.

on the Sea Islands," an article that appeared in the *Atlantic Monthly* in May 1864: "On every face there was a look of serenity and cheerfulness. My heart gave a great throb of happiness as I looked at them, and thought, 'They are free! So long down-trodden, so long crushed to the earth, but now in their old homes, forever free!' And I thanked God that I had lived to see this day."

Grimké and two other teachers from Philadelphia held classes for one hundred students every day in the Central Baptist Church. They taught a regular curriculum to the children during the day, and tutored the adults in reading and spelling in the evening. The school was named the Penn Normal School. It became an important part of the community for the students and their parents, who were mostly Gullah.

Grimké quickly became an active member of the community and worked with prominent leaders in the antislavery movement. On January 31, 1863, not long after President Lincoln signed the Emancipation Proclamation that freed the South's slaves, Grimké spent the day at the Beaufort, South Carolina, home of abolitionist Harriet Tubman. Known as the "Moses" of her people for her work on the Underground Railroad, Tubman conducted between 11 and 15 trips into the South to rescue more than 200 slaves and deliver them to freedom. Since conductors did not keep written records of their trips, the exact numbers are not known. Later, during the Civil War years, Tubman scouted for the Union Army. Tubman entertained Grimké and her other guests with stories of her Underground Railroad days. Grimké wrote in her journal: "How exciting it was to hear her tell the story. And to hear her sing the very scraps of jubilant hymns that he [a slave Tubman conducted to freedom] sang. She said the ladies crowded around them, and some laughed and some cried. My own eyes were full as I listened to her—the heroic woman!"

Grimké returned to Philadelphia in May 1864 due to ill health, but she continued her advocacy work promoting education in the Black community. By the late 1860s, Grimké had, through her numerous writings and lectures, made a name for herself among the abolitionists and the Black elite. She worked with several women's groups and Black advocates. She wrote of her experiences to point out to Black and White people alike the achievements Black Americans made in spite of overwhelming injustices.

In the twilight of the Civil War and emancipation, Africana women were bursting with the purpose and resolve of freedom—something that hitherto had been denied them, but which they then could embrace. ☥

With her step on the ice,
   and her arm on her child,
The danger was fearful,
   the pathway was wild....
But she's free! yes, free from
   the land where the slave,
From the hand of oppression,
   must rest in the grave.

—from "She's Free!"
   by Frances Ellen Watkins Harper

4 making a place in the world

Brown girl chanting Te Deums on Sunday
Rust-colored peasant with strength of granite,
Bronze girl wielding ship hulls on Monday,
Let nothing smirch you, let no one crush you.

—from "Ruth," by Pauli Murray

W hen slavery was abolished in the United States in 1865 with the ratification of the 13th Amendment, the fight for freedom was won; still, the fight for basic rights would continue well into the 20th century. In 1868 the 14th Amendment extended citizenship rights to African Americans. Through the first decade of the 1900s, Africana women worked to forge a foundation for the future success of all Black women and men.

Among those setting the pace were women like Frances E. W. Harper, a leader in the antislavery and suffrage movements. She became an internationally recognized journalist, the 19th century's most prolific African-American novelist, and America's best-loved African-American poet, known as the "bronze muse."

Born Frances Ellen Watkins in 1825 to a Baltimore, Maryland, family of free Black people, Harper was schooled at the prestigious Academy of Negro Youth in Baltimore. She studied Greek, Latin, and the Bible. Her education, excellent for a woman of any color or class of the time, provided a strong foundation for her life's goals of promoting high moral purpose and dedication to social service, but after graduation she could only find work as a babysitter and seamstress. In 1850 Harper chose to accept a teaching position in Ohio. She became the first female faculty member at Union Seminary—which later merged with Wilberforce University, the nation's first historically Black institute of higher learning. Eventually she moved to Philadelphia, Pennsylvania, where she lived with the Black abolitionist William Still and his family. Still's house was a stop on the Underground Railroad. Here Harper was exposed to the daily horrors of slavery, as well as when she frequented local antislavery offices and heard stories of cruel treatment of slaves in the South.

In 1854, Maryland passed a law saying that any Black person entering the state from

457. Cotton Pickers, Florida.

In the Office of the Librarian of Congress, at Washington.

Ranging in age from young to elderly, a group of cotton pickers in Florida took time out for a portrait in 1879. By this time, approximately three-quarters of Black people still living in the South supported themselves by farming, either as wage laborers or sharecroppers. Many women refused to return to the fields after the Civil War, however, choosing instead to stay home with their children.

Frances E. W. Harper.

the North could be sold into slavery. Harper was appalled; she took up the mantle of activist, lending her oratory skills to the antislavery movement. An articulate and impassioned speaker, she became one of the first African-American women abolitionist lecturers. Both the Maine Anti-Slavery Society and the Philadelphia Anti-Slavery Society sent her on lecture tours. She traveled throughout New England, Michigan, Ohio, and southern Canada, holding the audiences spellbound with such fiery words as those from an 1857 speech entitled "Liberty for Slaves": "I stand at the threshold of the Supreme Court and ask for justice, simple justice. Upon my tortured heart is thrown the mocking words. 'You are a Negro; you have no rights which white men are bound to respect'!"

In 1860, Frances Watkins married Fenton Harper and dedicated the next few years to raising children and living on a farm in Ohio—a much different life than the one to which she had become accustomed. Still the fire of her convictions burned. She returned to the lecture circuit shortly before Fenton died in 1864.

The title of her well-known poem, "We Are All Bound Up Together," espouses Harper's beliefs in life. She worked with the American Equal Rights Association, believing that its mission—"Equal Rights to all American citizens, especially the right of suffrage, irrespective of race, color, or sex"—dovetailed with her beliefs. In 1867, however, she found herself out of harmony with her counterparts, Elizabeth Cady Stanton, Susan B. Anthony, and other White feminists, who used racist and disparaging remarks about Black men in their fight to stop the passage of the 15th Amendment. It gave Black men the right to vote before women. Harper chose to side against the White women. Although she believed in equal rights for all, she could not stand in the way of progress for Black men.

Harper spoke passionately about Black self-determination. In her 1875 essay, "The Great Problem to be Solved," she wrote, "As fellow citizens, leaving out all humanitarian views—as a mere matter of political economy it is better to have the colored race a living force animated and strengthened by self-reliance and self-respect, than a stagnant mass, degraded and self-condemned.... Give power and significance to your own life, and in the great work of upbuilding there is room for women's work and woman's heart."

More than anything , Harper believed in the power and advancement of women—all women. In 1893 she addressed the World's Congress of Representative Women in Chicago:

Through weary, wasting years men have destroyed, dashed in pieces, and overthrown, but today we stand on the threshold of woman's era, and woman's work is grandly constructive.... The social and political advancement which woman has already gained bears the promise of the full-orbed sun of emancipation.... The ballot in the hands of woman means power added to influence. How well she will use that power I can not foretell. Great evils stare us in the face that need to be throttled by the combined power of an upright manhood and an enlightened womanhood; and I know that no nation can gain its full measure of enlightenment and happiness if one-half of it is free and the other half fettered.

Harper worked tirelessly for women's rights up until her death in 1911. She belonged to or helped establish more than seven clubs or organizations that advocated the advancement of women, including the American Woman Suffrage Association, the Universal Peace Union, the National Association of Colored Women, and the National Colored Women's Congress. She made an indelible mark on the Black woman's fight for equal rights. Her words resonated across the country and her leadership and passionate nature motivated a generation of women and had a profound impact on generations of women to come.

A contemporary of Frances Harper who left her signature on wartime and post-war Washington, D.C., was Elizabeth Keckley. Her entrepreneurship set an example for women of the 20th century. Through hard work and good fortune, Keckley became the personal maid and dressmaker of First Lady Mary Todd Lincoln. A prime job for any woman during this time, whether Black or White, Keckley secured the position after purchasing her freedom from slavery.

Keckley's saga is one of ingenuity and perseverance. Keckley was born a slave in 1818 in Dinwiddie Courthouse, Virginia. Her early life was marked by beatings and rapes—one of which resulted in the birth of her son, George—but her spirit was never broken. In the early 1850s, Keckley and her mother moved with their owners, the Garlands, to St. Louis, Missouri. When the household finances were so dire that Mr. Garland considered selling Keckley's mother, Keckley volunteered to work as a seamstress. Exceptionally gifted, she rarely lacked for clients. Indeed, she became a popular modiste for St. Louis society women. The income from her sewing covered the basic needs for all 17 members of the Garland household, including her mother, son, and husband, for more than two years.

Elizabeth Keckley, best known as dressmaker and close friend to Mary Todd Lincoln, defied society's limits of race and gender. She bought her freedom and pursued a life of her own making.

Opposite: "Let me make the songs for the people," wrote Frances E. W. Harper, photographed here for the frontispiece to her 1895 novel Iola Leroy. A prolific writer and talented speaker, Harper's words touched a chord with African-American women.

Georgia, Talbot County.

To any ordained Minister of the Gospel, Jewish Rabbi, Judge, Justice of the Inferior Court, or Justice of the Peace:

YOU ARE HEREBY AUTHORIZED

To join _Charles Gilbert (freedman)_ and _Susan Marshall (freedwoman)_

IN THE HOLY STATE OF

MATRIMONY,

According to the Constitution and Laws of this State, and for which this shall be your sufficient License.

21st day of _Dec._ 1866

Marion Bethune Ordinary.

_____, _Talbot_ County.

_____ Gilbert freedman _____ freedwoman were duly joined in ____ of _December_ 1866

John Pye J. P.

Printed at the Office of the West Georgia Gazette, Talbotton, Ga.

Keckley very much desired freedom, but she chose not to escape; as she saw it, she would only be truly free "by such means as the laws of the country provide." Mr. Garland, in return for Keckley's faithful service to his family, told Keckley she could buy her and her son's freedom for $1,200. In 1855, hearing of her desires for freedom, Keckley's patrons proffered Keckley the necessary money, but pride let her accept the money only as a loan. She worked herself nearly to ill health in order to pay back each of the ladies.

In 1860, Keckley left her husband of eight years—she had been unsatisfied with the marriage—and ventured to Baltimore, Maryland, and shortly thereafter to Washington, D.C. She had heard about Washington's active free Black community and the better opportunities it offered for entrepreneurship. In short order, Keckley succeeded in setting herself up as a dressmaker: "I rented apartments in a good locality, and soon had a good run of custom." One of her first clients was Varina Howell Davis, the wife of Senator Jefferson Davis, who recommended her to other society women. Keckley's skill with the needle quickly established her as one of the most popular dressmakers for the White elite. As the demand for her services grew, Keckley opened a shop; in time she employed up to 20 young women. Keckley's patrons considered her a beautiful woman who had a great talent for dressmaking and for managing a successful business.

Not long after Keckley arrived in Washington, Mrs. McClean, the daughter of General Sumner, introduced her to Mary Todd Lincoln, who loved the dress Keckley made for her. Shortly after meeting Mrs. Lincoln, Keckley became the First Lady's only designer and fashion consultant; she was frequently called to the White House to "dress" Mrs. Lincoln for the evening.

Mindful of her good fortune and aware of the horrors of war and the plight of her people, Keckley co-founded the Contraband Relief Association in 1862. The idea presented itself to her on a summer evening when she passed a garden ablaze with lights and buzzing with band music and people dancing, which turned out to be a benefit raising funds for the wounded. "If the white people can give festivals to raise funds for the relief of suffering soldiers, why should not the well-to-do colored people go to work to do something for the benefit of the suffering blacks?" wrote Keckley. "I made a suggestion to the colored church that a society of colored people be formed to labor for the benefit of the unfortunate freedmen. The idea proved popular." Mrs. Lincoln supported Keckley in her endeavors by contributing $200 to the association.

Keckley's friendship with Mrs. Lincoln blossomed over the years. "Lizzie," as the First Lady called her, became Mrs. Lincoln's trusted confidante and was privy to many

An 1866 marriage certificate affirms the union of an African-American couple. During and immediately after the Civil War, emancipated slaves rushed to legalize their marriages with ceremony and certificate because, at long last, they could. In one of the earliest known photographs (inset) of an African-American wedding celebration, dated about 1860, a bride and groom pose with loved ones. To have their marriages respected by law and White society was a privilege denied Black people during slavery.

private conversations between the President and Mrs. Lincoln. Keckley offered her opinion to Mrs. Lincoln on several matters when asked, and she sometimes accompanied Mrs. Lincoln on trips to New York and Boston. The two women shared their common grief in losing their sons, Keckley in 1861 and Mrs. Lincoln in 1863. After President Lincoln was assassinated on April 14, 1865, Keckley stood by the First Lady's side—called there by a woman in need of a trusted friend.

After Mrs. Lincoln moved to Chicago, Keckley needed to build up a new clientele. Although her reputation was solid, Keckley's business was slow to take hold, and she found her fortunes taking a downturn in 1868. She decided to write a book about her life—*Behind the Scenes or Thirty Years a Slave, and Four Years in the White House*—to make money for herself. Inadvertently, Keckley offended her greatest patron by revealing too many of the First Lady's secrets. Mrs. Lincoln ceased to communicate with Keckley. She did not appreciate Keckley announcing that at the time of Lincoln's death she was some $70,000 in debt to creditors and that her financial situation did not improve in the years afterward. The Lincolns' son Robert particularly despised what Keckley had written and he set out to destroy her.

The book stirred up strong reactions. White people believed Keckley had turned on one of their own, and African Americans believed Keckley had undermined their integrity, making it harder for White people to trust them and give them work. Needless to say, Keckley's business declined further.

In 1892, Keckley left Washington for Ohio, where she took a job at Wilberforce University teaching domestic arts. She never regained prominence or financial stability. She retired to the Home for Destitute Women and Children in Washington, D.C.—a home she earlier had helped establish—where she died in 1907. Although perhaps best known for the great uproar her tell-all book caused, Keckley performed good deeds that helped many individuals find a dignity and purpose that had been missing in their lives as slaves.

Unlike Keckley, who managed to buy her freedom and earn a livelihood, some slave women felt they would never find their fortune or their freedom if they stayed on the East Coast of the United States. The possibility of a better life in the western territories beckoned. As diaries, letters, and census data from the time reveal, many slaves accompanied families migrating west; other Black people, some free, others enslaved, made their way west with fur-trading expeditions, exploration teams, and military troops. Many of the western territories were more liberal than the southern states and were forming to enter

Six generations of Black women sat for a portrait in Selma, Alabama, at the close of the 19th century. Through the years of slavery and in its aftermath, Black women found strength in community. They saw each other through childbirth and sickness, helped raise each other's children, and gave comfort through friendship. As newly freed Black men and women struggled to provide for their families, support from the Black community remained as essential as ever.

the United States as free states, which gave Black people their civil rights. Many Black women were able to gain their freedom once they were in these territories, but they were still forced to work at low-paying and exhausting jobs, primarily domestic and agricultural tasks. Mary Ellen Smith Pleasant, entrepreneur and civil rights activist, was one of the few exceptions.

Pleasant related so many accounts of her life that it is not easy to separate fact from fiction—which only adds to her mystique. The question of her birth—where, when, and even to whom—remains a matter of debate among historians, but some aspects of her life can be confirmed. She was born in the 1810s and was indentured to a Quaker merchant in Nantucket, Massachusetts. In 1841, when her service ended, she moved to Boston.

She worked as a tailor's assistant and became involved with the Underground Railroad. She met William Lloyd Garrison and other abolitionists, including Cuban planter Alexander Smith, whom she married. Upon his death, sometime in the mid-1840s, Smith willed Pleasant $45,000, making her a very wealthy woman. Smith intended that she use the money to further the abolitionist cause—and she did. She worked with Mary Ann Shadd Cary, Martin Delaney, and John James Pleasant, who would become her second husband, helping fugitive slaves to freedom. As a result, around 1849 she was forced to flee New

England; she eventually joined her new husband, who also had to leave New England for his safety, in San Francisco. The California gold rush was in full swing.

Pleasant continued her abolitionist work in California, as well as in Canada, where she reportedly moved in the late 1850s. At some point, she left Canada and returned east to offer moral and financial support to the abolitionists. She supported the radical abolitionist John Brown, allegedly giving him $30,000. After the raid on Harpers Ferry failed in 1859, Brown was hanged and Pleasant narrowly escaped a similar fate—she fled back west under an assumed name.

Back in San Francisco, Pleasant became an entrepreneur and investor—and throughout the Civil War she illegally assisted fugitive slaves. She ran several laundries and eating establishments, including a restaurant at 920 Washington Street, in the heart of today's Chinatown. This popular restaurant was nicknamed the "Black City Hall" because Pleasant used it as an informal employment agency for Black people: They knew they could go there to find work. Her business acumen and access to ready labor contributed to her rise to power as one of San Francisco's "city bosses."

Throughout the rest of her life, she continued to demand equal civil rights for Black people. One of her most important victories came in 1863—the same year as the Emancipation Proclamation—with the passage of the California law that gave Black Americans the right to testify in court. In 1868 she challenged the Jim Crow laws in her landmark case against the North Beach Railroad Company for refusing to allow her to board a streetcar. She won $500 in damages. The case, however, was appealed.

Pleasant's business success led many people to cast aspersions on her. She was called defamatory names. She was accused of being a voodoo queen and using magic powers to garner her success. But Pleasant never let these accusations distract her from her life's work fighting for civil rights. She was exceedingly proud of her abolitionist work and, before she died in 1904, she requested that her gravestone mention that she was a friend of John Brown.

Another woman making a name for herself in California around the same time as Pleasant was Bridget "Biddy" Mason. Mason ran several thriving boardinghouses before becoming a successful real estate broker and one of the most celebrated figures of late 19th-century Los Angeles. Born into slavery in Hancock, Mississippi, in 1818, Mason was believed to be of African and mixed-Indian descent. Early in life, she learned to be a midwife and a medicine woman, practicing the secrets passed down from her ancestors. When she was 18, she was given to Robert and Rebecca Smith as a wedding present. When the

Opposite: Biddy Mason, a woman of remarkable heart and achievement, bought this house in Los Angeles. While a slave, she had walked almost all the way from Mississippi to California, where she sued for her freedom and won. She later amassed a small fortune, which she used within the Black community, especially to help struggling families.

A poster distributed by Benjamin "Pap" Singleton, a former slave who had made one too many coffins for Black people murdered by White people, urged Black people to move west. Thousands heeded the call, joining the so-called "exoduster" movement.

Smiths converted to Mormonism and decided to head west to Utah in 1848, Biddy and her three children, reportedly Smith's, accompanied them. Biddy walked at the rear of the wagon train, herding the cattle.

In 1851, the Smiths relocated to San Bernardino, California—in all likelihood Smith forgot, or didn't realize, that a year earlier California had been declared a free state. When the Smiths attempted to relocate to Texas in 1855, Mason petitioned the California courts for her and her children's freedom. Mason and her children were unknowingly fortunate. They were manumitted on January 1, 1856, just a year before the Dred Scott case ruling that effectively stated "once a slave, always a slave." Seeking a better life, Mason and her children moved to Los Angeles, where she worked as a nurse and midwife.

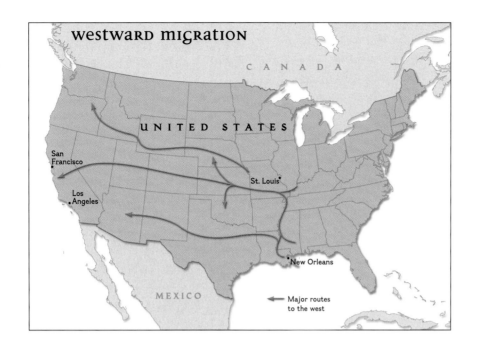

westward migration

The Shores family, outside their Nebraska homestead in 1897 (below), and 50,000 other African Americans followed the dusty wagon trail west between 1878 and 1881 (map). Most lacked the basics needed to establish a homestead. Still they persevered, seeking a better life in the West. "Stagecoach Mary" Fields (opposite) found work as a handywoman, restaurant owner, and U.S. stagecoach driver in Montana Territory.

Truth and Grace Hannah display a prize catch outside their Nebraska home after a successful fishing trip at the turn of the 20th century. Self-sufficiency was the key to survival in the West, as most Black settlers learned. They had to build their own houses, fashion their own farm tools, make their own furniture, and provide their own food—which meant growing it, shooting it, or catching it. While most females made the long, hard journey west in the company of their families, some went as "mail-order brides." They assumed the roles of homemaker and mother, as well as domestic, farmworker, cook, seamstress, innkeeper, laundress, general store manager, teacher, and nurse.

According to some accounts, Mason would travel the length of Southern California—from San Diego to Santa Barbara—to render aid to her clients in jails and hospitals. As Biddy was known to say, "If you hold your hand closed, nothing good can come in. The open hand is blessed, for it gives in abundance, even as it receives." She was held in high esteem and considered an angel of mercy to those in need.

After ten years of frugal living, Mason was able to purchase a home for her family on Spring Street in downtown Los Angeles, making her the first Black female property owner in Los Angeles. As her earnings from nursing grew, Mason invested in properties that she turned into boardinghouses; she earned a substantial income from the rents. The area in which she invested was fast turning into the city's downtown. A devout woman, Mason financed the establishment of the First African Methodist Episcopal Church in Los Angeles. Following her death in 1891, her investments made her family the wealthiest among Black people in Los Angeles at the turn of the 20th century.

Another wealthy woman who used her good fortune to help others was Clara Brown. Born into slavery in Virginia in 1800, Brown's early life was marked by sorrow. She was separated at an early age from her mother and taken to Kentucky; and she was separated later from her own three children, who were all sold to different owners. In 1835, Brown became the property of George Brown. A kind man, he tried to help her find her children, but to no avail. George Brown died in 1855, and his daughters gave Clara Brown her freedom. In order to remain free, she had to leave Kentucky. In 1859, she decided to go west in search of riches when she heard of a gold rush occurring that year in Colorado.

Brown paid for her journey west by working as a cook on an eight-week-long wagon-train trip to Denver, Colorado. She is said to be the first Black woman to cross the plains during the gold rush. She settled in Denver for a little while before moving to Central City, a booming miner's camp some 35 miles west of the city. The camp offered plenty of opportunity for enterprising souls. Brown established the camp's first laundry, washing shirts for 50 cents apiece. A deeply Christian woman, Brown turned her home into a boardinghouse for the needy; she rarely turned anyone away for lack of coin. She also held church services in her home and started the camp's first Sunday school. Over the years she invested in several lucrative mining claims, which, by the end of the Civil War, earned her a tidy fortune of $10,000—enough to look for her family back East.

Unable to find any of her children, Brown returned to Colorado with 16 freedmen and -women. She paid their passage, as she wanted as many freed slaves as possible to enjoy the prosperity and opportunities that she experienced. She financed several wagon trains to bring African Americans from the South to the West. Among the groups were 34 of her relatives; unfortunately, none were her children. It wasn't until 1882 that she found her daughter Eliza Jane, who had been living in Iowa.

Clara Brown died in 1885 at the age of 85 and was buried with honors by the Colorado Pioneers Association, an organization in which she held membership for a number of years (she was the organization's first Black member). She was, according to the Colorado Pioneers Association, "the kind of old friend whose heart always responded to the cry of distress and who, rising from the humble position of slave to the angelic type of noblewoman, won our sympathy and commanded our respect."

A woman who commanded respect of a different nature altogether was Mary Fields. Her pioneering spirit and colorful personality made her a legend out West, where, late in her life, she became the first female United States mail carrier. This feat earned her the moniker "Stagecoach Mary."

Fields was born a slave in Hickman County, Tennessee, in the 1830s. The circumstances of her life after that are relatively unknown until 1884, at which point Fields, then around 50 years old, lived in Toledo, Ohio, and worked at an Ursuline convent. Fields knew the mother superior, Amadeus, from earlier days when Fields was owned by the mother superior's family; the two women established a lasting friendship. When Fields learned that Mother Amadeus contracted pneumonia while setting up a mission in Montana, Fields journeyed nearly 2,000 miles so she could nurse her friend back to good health.

Afterward, Fields decided to stay out West. At first she performed odd jobs that were in keeping with "women's work"—cleaning, farming, gardening—but after a time she started doing "men's work": working construction at the convent and driving the supply wagon to and from town. Montana was not the easiest place to live; Fields needed her wits to survive. When the supply wagon became disabled in the middle of nowhere one sub-zero night, Fields walked back and forth all night to keep from freezing to death.

Some townspeople were shocked by her actions, and more so by her appearance. She stood six feet tall, weighed 200 pounds, and wore men's clothing. She even acted like a man: She smoked cigars, drank in saloons, swore, and fought with men. She had a temper and, by many accounts, was quite ornery. News of Fields's exploits soon reached Bishop Brondel, Mother Amadeus's superior. Outraged and believing Fields gave the mission a bad name, he insisted that Mother Amadeus get rid of Fields.

Fields met with the bishop to allay his concerns, but to no avail. The mother superior had no choice but to obey the bishop. After a series of failed enterprises, Fields, then

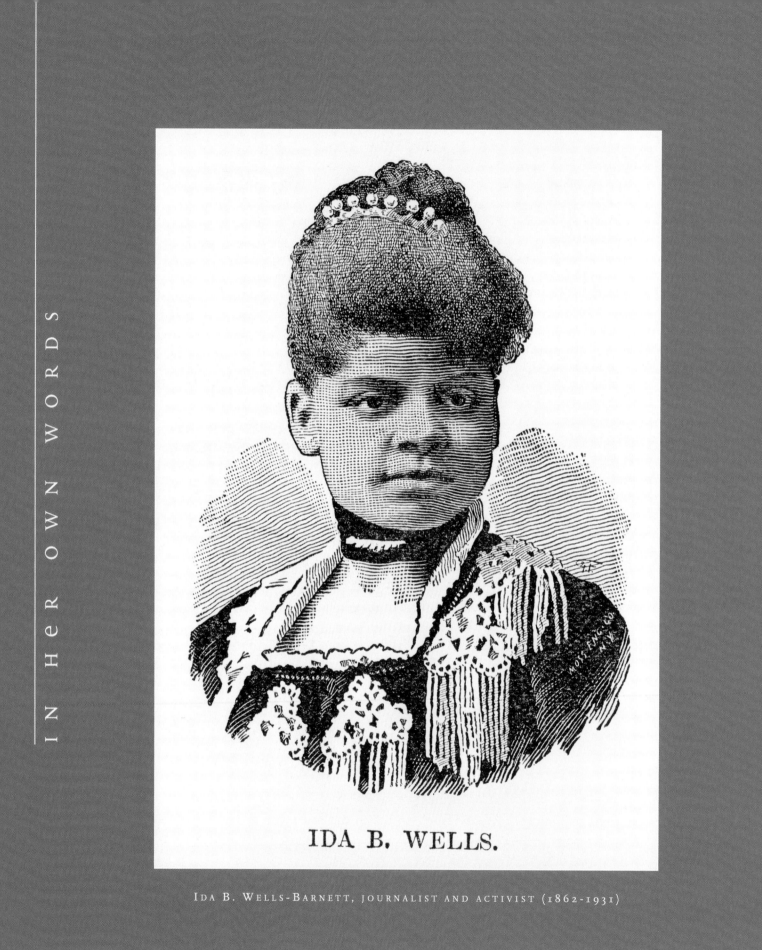

IDA B. WELLS.

IDA B. WELLS-BARNETT, JOURNALIST AND ACTIVIST (1862-1931)

Ida B. Wells-Barnett

In A Red Record, Wells-Barnett's statistics disproved the Southern argument that lynching responded to Black assaults on White women. Her missive ended with this:

What can you do to prevent lynching and promote law and order...?

1. Let the facts [in this book] speak for themselves, with you as a medium.

2. ...be instrumental in having churches, ...YMCAs and all Christian and moral forces...pass resolutions of condemnation every time a lynching takes place.

3. Bring to the...Southern people the refusal of capital to invest where lawlessness and mob violence hold sway.

4. Think and act on independent lines... remembering that after all, it is the white man's civilization and the white man's government which are on trial.

JUBILEE SINGERS

MAGGIE PORTER.   E. W. WATKINS.   H. D. ALEXANDER.   F. J. LOUDIN.   THOMAS RUTLING.
JENNIE JACKSON.   MABEL LEWIS.   ELLA SHEPPARD.   MAGGIE CARNES.   AMERICA W. ROBINSON.

past 60 years old, turned to the U.S. postal service. Hired to deliver the mail, she was based out of Cascade, Montana. Traveling the territory was hard, dangerous work, but Fields never shirked her duty. She even would strap on snowshoes and deliver the mail by foot to the residents along her route. In addition to the mail, she transported travelers and their luggage, making her the first Black woman stagecoach driver—and earning her the nickname "Stagecoach Mary."

When Fields retired from her job, she was well over 70 years old. She settled in Cascade. She was the only African American in town. By then her exploits were legendary and the townspeople had grown to accept and respect her. The former servant from Tennessee became a town treasure. When the laundry that she ran burned down, all the townspeople helped her finance and rebuild a new establishment. She died in 1914, an example of a strong Black woman living a life of her own choice.

throughout the U.S., especially in the South and East, Black women fought for basic civil rights. Ida Bell Wells-Barnett made her mark on the world by exposing the plight of Black people in the Deep South. She publicized through written and spoken word the horror of lynchings, calling attention to the inhumane act and forcing people across the country to acknowledge its occurrence and the discrimination that was at its root.

Born Ida Bell Wells in Holly Springs, Mississippi, in 1862, Wells-Barnett grew up in the postbellum South. Her parents had lived in harsh circumstances during slavery; they were determined to see their children have a better existence, and they believed education was the key to success. Emancipated Black people in the 1860s were free to be formally educated: They sent their children to school. The intelligent Wells-Barnett continued her education beyond grammar school. She attended Shaw's new institute for higher learning. When her parents died in 1878, she took and passed a teacher's examination so she could support her younger siblings. Although Wells-Barnett's teaching job was a source of pride for herself and her family, the pay was very low—only $25 a month. She and her siblings moved to Memphis, Tennessee, to live with their aunt. Wells-Barnett secured a teaching job in the Shelby County school district. A few years later, an incident occurred that changed her life forever.

It was May 1884. Wells-Barnett, with two of her younger sisters, boarded the ladies' coach of a Chesapeake and Ohio train. The conductor informed them they must move to the forward segregated coach. Wells-Barnett refused: "As I was in the ladies' car, I proposed to stay." She and the conductor scuffled and she was forcibly removed from the train, along with her sisters. Wells-Barnett immediately hired a Black lawyer and sued the railroad company on the grounds that it refused her the first-class carriage even though she had a first-class ticket. Disappointed by her lawyer's lack of commitment to the case, she hired a White lawyer. He successfully argued her case and Wells-Barnett was awarded $500 in 1884. Unfortunately, in 1887 the state supreme court reversed the judgment of the lower court on appeal, saying that the railroad had satisfied the statutory requirements by providing "like accommodations." Incensed by the court's action, Wells-Barnett detailed her experiences in her first journalistic outing—an article in the Living Way, a religious weekly. From that moment on, Wells-Barnett became an ardent advocate for civil, economic, and women's rights.

In 1891 Wells-Barnett stopped teaching and committed herself full-time to a career in journalism, which she had taken up in 1889 when she became an editor and co-owner of the Memphis Free Speech and Headlight. In 1892, a mob shot and hanged three close friends and colleagues of hers in Memphis. Appalled by the lawlessness of the act, Wells-Barnett

This photograph of the Jubilee Singers of Fisk University was taken in 1875, the same year the student choral group toured England and performed for Queen Victoria. The group from the newly founded Black university in Nashville made its singing debut only four years earlier. Although they performed many types of music, the Jubilee Singers became famous for the spirituals and work songs that they sang, many of which were unknown to White audiences. The group still performs today.

became an outspoken antilynching activist. She drew national attention to the barbaric practice of lynching in her many articles that appeared in newspapers around the country. Her descriptions—which didn't spare the gruesome details—moved people to act against the practice. The articles brought her notoriety and danger: Wells-Barnett was threatened and her newspaper offices were burned down that same year. Wells-Barnett left the South for Chicago, but she wouldn't give in to the scare tactics. She continued to write and campaign for antilynching laws.

In 1895 she authored A Red Record, a definitive statistical work on lynching in the United States that disproved the Southern argument that lynching was a means by which to combat Black assaults on White women. The book launched a national antilynching campaign and Wells-Barnett led the legal efforts to prevent lynchings. That same year, Ida Wells married Ferdinand L. Barnett, an editor and lawyer. She toned down her rhetoric while she was busy raising children, but when media attention would waver, Wells-Barnett would appeal to the Black community to rally in support of the Anti-Lynching Bureau. In 1902 she wrote:

> Time was when the country resounded with denunciation and the horror of burning a human being by so called Christian and civilized people. The newspapers were full of it. The last time a human being was made fuel for flames it was scarcely noticed in the papers editorially. And the chairman of your bureau finds it harder every year to get such matter printed. In other words, the need for agitation and publication of facts is greater than ever, while the avenues through which to make such publications have decreased…. We can only change public sentiment and enforce laws by educating the people, giving them facts.

Wells-Barnett never backed down from her beliefs. She co-founded the National Association for the Advancement of Colored People in 1909 with W. E. B. Du Bois, and also was a leading exponent of the Black suffrage movement. She "believed agitation, activism, and protest were the only means of change in the U.S." This belief would be echoed by her generation's daughters, who were on the frontlines of the Civil Rights Movement of the mid-1900s. ⚲

Carlotta Stewart-Lai, a respected teacher in Hawaii for more than 40 years, used her education and talents to her advantage. A native of Brooklyn, New York, she made Hawaii her home, knowing that there the color of her skin would not be held against her.

Following pages: An afternoon pageant at Griffith Stadium in Washington, D.C., at the turn of the 20th century, attracts African-American socialites. Nellie Quander, first supreme basileus of Alpha Kappa Alpha, the first sorority for Black women in America, stands fourth from left in the row of parasol-toting ladies.

But there remain large countries
    in your eyes.
Shrewd sun.
The civil balance.
The listening secrets.
And you create and train your
    flowers still.

—from "To Black Women,"
    by Gwendolyn Brooks

5 taking society by storm

A white woman has only one handicap
to overcome—a great one, true, her sex;
a colored woman faces two—her sex
and her race.

—Mary Church Terrell

In the late 1800s, the United States—especially the South—was a place of great turmoil for Black people. Reconstruction had ended in 1877, stopping all federally funded social services; lynchings were rampant; and discriminatory Jim Crow laws were firmly in place in many states. The rights Black people had won after emancipation—embodied in the 14th and 15th Amendments—were being eroded by a growing sentiment of White supremacy. In 1896, the U.S. Supreme Court ruled in *Plessy v. Ferguson* that "separate but equal" treatment was constitutional, thus legalizing segregation and virtually relegating Black people to second-class citizenship.

To help the Black race rise up from these downtrodden beginnings as free people in the U.S., and to prosper in a deeply segregated U.S., educated Black men and women traveled throughout the South and East, working to improve the lives of Black people and speaking out on how education was the key to success. There were different opinions within the Black community, though, on the best type of education needed to succeed.

Educator, sociologist, and historian W. E. B. Du Bois—the first Black person to obtain a doctorate degree from Harvard University and later a founder of the National Association for the Advancement of Colored People (NAACP)—promoted the ideal of the Talented Tenth. Briefly, Du Bois called for the education and leadership development of promising Black men and women—every tenth person—so these men and women could lead and inspire the remaining nine-tenths of Black society. Du Bois explained his philosophy in the 1903

African-American children sew paper leaves in an arts-and-crafts class at their Washington, D.C., public elementary school in 1899. The curriculum for most Black students at the time balanced academic subjects like reading, writing, and arithmetic with practical vocational training.

Preceding pages: Four stylish friends turn heads on Seventh Avenue in 1936. At the time, this grand boulevard of Black Harlem was the place to see and be seen. Especially on Sunday afternoons, recalled one resident, "you didn't want to be caught dressed sloppily on Seventh Avenue!"

book, *The Negro Problem*, which was a collection of articles written by African Americans. Du Bois believed Black people had the same inalienable rights as White people. He felt strongly that Black people needed to fight for those rights to institute social change.

Booker T. Washington, the head of Tuskegee Institute, advocated a fundamentally different approach to social change. Washington believed Black people were due the same rights as White people, but that Black people needed to be more accommodating in order to gain those rights. His position did not challenge the status quo; it advocated acceptance as the means to successful integration. Through hard work and diligence Black people would earn their rights—and prove themselves worthy. Washington encouraged Black people to get industrial and domestic-type training—a "useful" education that would put them into the American workforce. His voice of conciliation resonated with millions of people—both Black and White. In fact, some Southern White people warmly received his message of conciliation; their support for the organizations and values he endorsed positioned Washington as the leading authority on racial affairs. His endorsement of industrial and domestic education caused it to be widely regarded, especially by White people, as the premier method of education for Black people. But education alone—whether Washington's approach or Du Bois's—was not sufficient to change the status of the masses.

There were other vital means of societal uplift. In 1818, a group of free Black women in Massachusetts established the Colored Female Religious and Moral Society of Salem. They charged their members to "be charitably watchful over each other." Over the next decades, African-American women established many mutual benefit societies, sororities—among them Delta Sigma Theta and Alpha Kappa Alpha—and other organizations to provide social services to needy Black populations. These self-help clubs gave women a forum where they could discuss issues that concerned them. At weekly get-togethers, the women could learn about educational programs and how to run a household, discuss child-rearing and health care, find moral support, and acquire financial aid.

As the clubs grew in stature and importance, especially after Reconstruction ended and the clubs were the sole source of help, they evolved from their humble beginnings to be the Black woman's voice. They championed women's rights and challenged the government and society for their due. The leaders of these organizations were highly educated, take-charge women. Most came from middle- and upper-middle-class backgrounds and had grown up instilled with a desire to help their people. As Black women in the early to mid-1900s strove to gain basic civil rights, and women's rights in general, a number of women came to the fore of the fight.

In this typescript written in the early 1900s, Mary Church Terrell, a founder and the first president of the National Association of Colored Women (NACW), assessed the impact of the NACW's work. In 1896 the NACW united several Black women's clubs that were dedicated to racial uplift. Terrell concludes that while the NACW had provided strength through organized effort, it would be misleading to suggest that Black women had not always striven for the betterment of themselves, their families, and their communities.

What the National Association Has Meant to Colored Women.

It would be hard to overestimate the splendid contribution which the National Association of Colored Women has made to the development of the group for which it was ~~organized~~ formed. When two national organizations merged in Washington, D.C. in 1896 and solidified the women ~~in~~ into one large body a new day for them had dawned. Their eyes were turned to duties which women alone can perform as they had never been turned before. They were ~~organized~~ pressed into doing certain kinds of work and were advised concerning the best methods with which to proceed. They were urged to interest themselves in civic affairs- to study the conditions under which they lived in their respective cities and towns and to do everything they could to put the right men into places of trust and power long before the amendment granting suffrage to women was passed.

And yet, it would misrepresent the facts to say that colored women had done little or nothing for themselves or their race until the National Association of Colored Women was formed. The rapidity with which colored women strode forward as soon as they were enfranchised would sound like a fairy tale if it were told. Unfortunately, it has not been written yet, but when it is, it will amaze the world.

Colored women have always had high aspirations for themselves and their race. From the day when shackles fell from their fettered limbs till to day, as ijdividuals they have often struggled single handed and alone against the most desperate and discouraging odds, in order to secure for themselves and their loved ones that culture of the head and heart for which they had hungered and thirsted so long inxvain. But it dawned upon them finally that individuals working alone, or scattered here and there in small companies, might be never so honest in purpose, so indefatigable in labor, so conscientious about methods and so wise in projecting plans, they would nevertheless accomplish little sompared with the possible achievements of many individuals, all banded strongly together throughout the entire land, with heads and hearts fixed on the same high purpose, and hands joined in united strength.

althInthough born in 1867 into a family of humble means, Maggie Lena Walker had the advantage of being born into freedom and its associated rights and privileges. She grew up in Richmond, Virginia. Her mother, having lost two husbands, was forced to become a laundress. It was one of the few occupations open to Black women and one that allowed her to work at home and care for her two young children. She pressed upon her children how important an education was to bettering their place in society. Maggie took her words to heart and excelled in her studies.

Maggie graduated from high school at the head of her class in 1883. Interested in business, she took night classes in accounting and business management while she taught primary grades at Richmond's Lancaster School during the day. She left teaching three years later, when she married Armstead Walker, and committed herself full-time to the Richmond chapter of the Independent Order of St. Luke, a mutual benefit society she had joined when she was 14 years old. Mutual benefit societies—the first ones founded by free Black people in the late 18th century—flourished in the Reconstruction era. In addition to providing financial aid, they aimed to promote the welfare of the Black community by encouraging education, financial responsibility, and self-reliance.

Walker worked tirelessly for the organization, teaching men and women how to manage their money and take responsibility for their future security. She encouraged women to go into business, to have self-confidence in their abilities. As she exclaimed in a speech at Richmond's Bethel A.M.E. Church in 1925, "If our women want to avoid the

traps and snares of life, they must band themselves together, organize, acknowledge leadership, put their hands and brains and mites together and make openings for themselves." Honoring her years of service, the Order named Walker the executive secretary of its Richmond chapter in 1889; ten years later, she headed the entire organization.

It was very difficult at the turn of the 20th century for Black people to obtain home and business loans. "Let us put our money together," Walker proposed in 1901. "Let us use our money; let us put our money out at usury among ourselves, and reap the benefit ourselves." She observed and studied the activities of the Merchant's National Bank of

Maggie Lena Walker stands with two male employees at the central teller's window of the St. Luke Penny Savings Bank, which she founded in 1903 in Richmond, Virginia. Working for a Black mutual benefit society known as the Order of St. Luke, Walker came to believe that penny by penny (opposite), the Black community could and should become economically independent of White people. "Brethren and sisters, let us awake," she exhorted in 1901. "Let us have a bank that will take the nickels and turn them into dollars. How easily then can [we] start to do good in our ranks."

Richmond to make it a reality. The St. Luke Penny Savings Bank opened its doors to the Order's members in 1903, with 37-year-old Walker in charge—the first female president of a charter bank in the United States. Walker was a savvy businesswoman with an aptitude for banking. The St. Luke bank prospered under Walker's guidance, even during the Great Depression when most banks folded. St. Luke's survived because the bank had recently restructured to focus on insurance, with most of its capital invested in secure bonds instead of business ventures. Hundreds of people benefited from her business insights.

Always diligent and ever mindful of the importance of education and self-help for Black women, Walker supported numerous organizations that promoted the Black woman's cause. In 1912 she founded the Council of Colored Women to serve the interests of Richmond's Black community. Under Walker's presidency the Council raised $5,000 for the Industrial school; it also bought a house that served as a canteen for World War II Black servicemen and as the Richmond chapter office of the NAACP. Black women's clubs and other groups loved her speaking style and motivational lectures. She traveled the country giving inspirational lectures on money matters, women's rights, and disfranchisement.

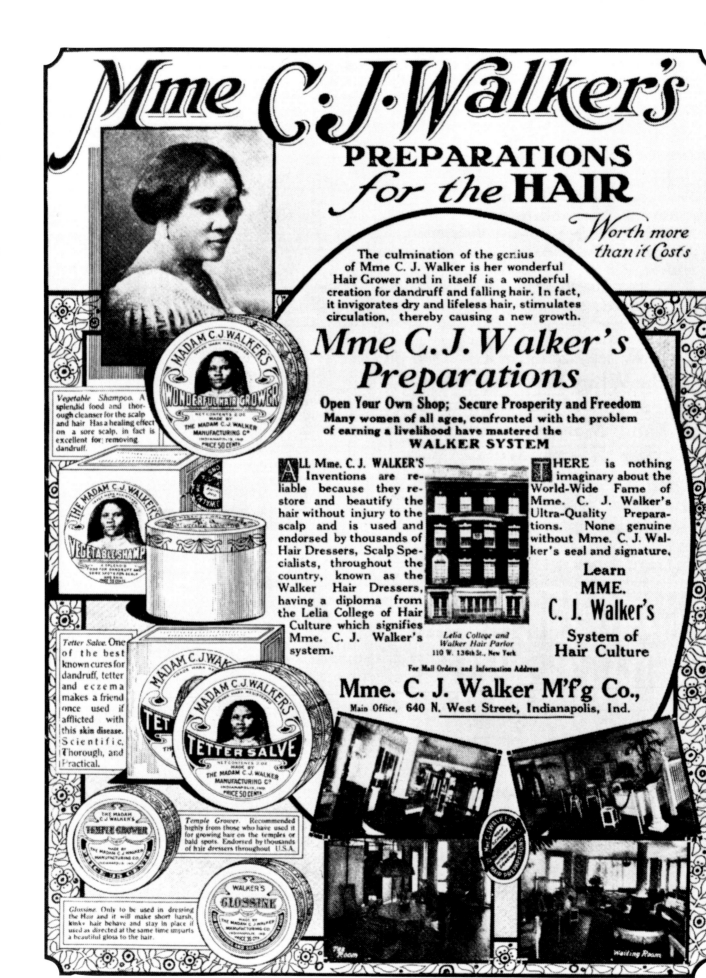

Even after diabetes confined her to a wheelchair, Walker remained a formidable advocate—earning her the nickname "the lame lioness." After being the guiding force behind the Independent Order of St. Luke's for 35 years—inspiring hundreds of women to better themselves through financial responsibility in the process—Walker died in 1934.

Around the same time that Maggie Lena Walker was prospering in her enterprises, Madam C. J. Walker was using her business acumen to run one of the most successful Black-owned businesses in the country. Like Maggie Walker, Madam C. J. Walker came from humble beginnings. She was born Sarah Breedlove in Delta, Louisiana, in 1867. Her parents were former slaves and cotton pickers. She married early and was a mother by the age of 17. At 21, she moved to St. Louis, Missouri, leaving behind her husband, and spent the next 14 years toiling as a washerwoman and cook. She longed for something better. Without any formal education, Walker relied upon self-improvement and self-promotion to achieve her end. Like many Black women, Walker suffered from alopecia (patchy baldness) due to poor diet, stress, scalp diseases, and damaging hair treatments. After finding some relief using a particular hair care product, Walker became an agent for the company—selling hair care products door to door—to supplement her laundress income. Walker was a born saleswoman. Soon she saw the hair care business as her salvation.

In 1905, she moved to Denver and continued selling for the company. But within a few months, she decided to go into business for herself. She changed the formula, persuaded several respected members of Denver's Black community to try her products and endorse them, then poured all the profits into advertising. The demand for her scalp treatments was overwhelming. In 1906, following her marriage to Charles Joseph Walker, she used the business title Madam C. J. Walker. She traveled the country promoting herself and her products, training sales agents, and advertising her mail-order operation in local newspapers. The business was a resounding success. To cope with the growth, she moved the company first to Pittsburgh, then Indianapolis, and finally New York City. In each location she increased her visibility in the Black community; with greater accessibility to shipping networks and ingredients, her profits rose. By 1913, the seven-year-old Madam C. J. Walker Manufacturing Company could claim 20,000 female sales agents, most of whom were making more money in one day than they were in one week working as a domestic or laundress.

"I got my start by giving myself a start," Madam Walker was fond of saying. And she gave starts to numerous others through her philanthropy. In 1911, she donated $1,000 to the construction of a YMCA for Black people in Indianapolis. Her gift, the largest given to the fundraising drive by a Black woman, received national attention, causing her name

An advertisement for Madam C. J. Walker's hair products (opposite) features the likeness of the ingenious laundress-turned-business tycoon. In 1917, 12 years after Walker launched her business, an army of dedicated "hair culturists" gathered for the company's first annual convention (badge, above). Walker was by then a wealthy woman who lived the part, but also applied her fortune "to help [her] race."

to become synonymous with philanthropy. The following year, Madam Walker attended the annual National Negro Business League; she wished to address the delegates, entrepreneur to entrepreneur. She faced stiff opposition from conference head Booker T. Washington, but she finally had her say by refusing to sit down.

> I have been trying to get before you business people and tell you what I am doing. I am a woman that came from the cotton fields of the South. I was promoted from there to the wash-tub. Then I was promoted to the cook kitchen, and from there I promoted myself into the business of manufacturing hair goods and preparations…. I have built my own factory on my own ground…. I own my own automobile and runabout…. Now my object in life is not simply to make money for myself or to spend it on myself in dressing or running around in an automobile. But I love to use a part of what I make in trying to help others.

Madam Walker used her philanthropy to make bold political statements, weighing in on causes affecting the welfare of all African Americans. She opened her Hudson River home for meetings of Black leaders and contributed $5,000 to an antilynching campaign sponsored by the NAACP. But more significant, perhaps, her philanthropy made education a possibility for hundreds of Black women and men. Generous to schools throughout her prosperous career, Madam Walker's generosity prevailed even upon her death in 1919: She willed one-third of her considerable estate—believed at that time by the public to be around one million dollars—to various charities and schools, including Mary McLeod Bethune's Daytona Educational and Industrial Institute. Madam C. J. Walker's can-do attitude inspired Black women—and men—to believe in themselves and what they could accomplish.

After the Civil War, more than 85 percent of the Black population could neither read nor write, but the desire to learn was strong. Women were at the forefront of education in the late 1800s. They were the overwhelming majority of educators at the primary and secondary levels. Most received their only schooling at Normal Schools. These were established in part by the Freedmen's Bureau to train students to be primary school teachers in order to standardize and raise the level of education offered to Black people. A small minority of women pursued a true collegiate education. They studied liberal arts and sciences at such places as Oberlin College, Spelman College, Wilberforce University, and Fisk University. Through education they empowered themselves—they became teachers, orators, women's leaders, activists, and, in the end, role models to future generations. Their influence stretched far and wide. One such woman was Anna Julia Cooper.

Anna Julia Hayward Cooper was born in 1858 in Raleigh, North Carolina, to a slave woman and her master. After the Civil War she was sent to school; she loved learning so much that she decided at a very early age to be a teacher. A precocious student, she entered at age ten the new and then-ungraded Saint Augustine's Normal School and Collegiate Institute in Raleigh. While at Saint Augustine's, she tutored other students, many of whom were much older . Several years later, she led a protest against the school when it allowed only ministerial students—therefore only men—to study Greek and Latin.

After graduating from St. Augustine's in the mid-1870s, Anna Julia joined its faculty. She married George A. G. Cooper, a ministerial student and fellow teacher, in June 1877. The Coopers' happiness was cut short, however, when George died in 1879. Anna Julia Cooper was a widow at the age of 21.

After a period of grieving, Cooper decided to pursue her education at Oberlin College. "I had devoured what was put before me, and, like Oliver Twist, was looking around to ask for more," she explained much later. "I constantly felt (as I suppose many an ambitious girl has felt) a thumping from within unanswered by any beckoning from without." Unlike most female students of the time, Cooper took the four-year "gentleman's course," which was a sophisticated Classics curriculum. She and fellow Oberlin students Mary Eliza Church (Terrell) and Ida Gibbs (Hunt) graduated in 1884—only the second, third, and fourth African-American women to receive a four-year bachelor's degree from an accredited American college.

Cooper accepted a teaching position at Wilberforce University, in Ohio, but she taught for only one year before returning to St. Augustine's Normal School in Raleigh to teach German, Latin, and mathematics. Cooper proved herself a gifted teacher—one who motivated and inspired her students to learn, achieve, and better themselves. Her reputation as a teacher grew. She taught by example: While at Wilberforce, she started to pursue a master's degree in mathematics from Oberlin College. She earned it by mail in 1887.

That year the superintendent of colored schools in Washington, D.C., convinced Cooper to join the staff of the M Street High School—the country's most prestigious African-American high school at the time. Rev. Alexander Crummell—a leading figure in the Black community and a noted abolitionist—and his wife were impressed by Cooper's accomplishments. They invited her to board with them. Cooper found herself in familiar

MARY CHURCH TERRELL, WOMEN'S RIGHTS ACTIVIST (1863-1954)

MARY CHURCH TERRELL

Educator and activist Terrell advanced the Black Women's
Club Movement to help women improve "their own
conditions and that of their race." She comments below:

The effort made by colored women to educate
and elevate themselves would read like
a fairy tale if it were written. But,
unfortunately for the race, it has not been
written. Ignorance for which the group was
not responsible, made it impossible for newly
emancipated slaves to keep a record....
From the day the colored woman's fetters
were broken, her mind released from
the darkness of ignorance in which it had
been held for nearly three hundred years
and she could stand erect in the dignity of
womanhood, no longer bond but free, till
this minute, generally speaking she has been
forging steadily ahead, acquiring knowledge
and exerting herself strenuously to promote
the welfare of the race.

Mary McLeod Bethune escorts students of the Daytona Educational and Industrial Institute for Negro Girls, the school that she founded in 1904 with only $1.50. By then, Bethune was an experienced teacher, having instructed her 16 siblings at home.

Opposite: Anna Julia Cooper— writer, scholar, lecturer, civil rights activist—was above all an educator. She respected the dignity and importance of women as mothers and homemakers, and believed that the best way to elevate Black women—to help them gain a voice of their own— was through higher education.

company: Fellow Oberlin graduates Mary Church and Ida Gibbs also lived with the Crummells. Cooper met distinguished members of Black society—Du Bois among them— through the Crummells. She got caught up in the self-help activism they advocated. Cooper and the other women worked for social progress in the Black community by establishing clubs for learning and culture.

In 1892 she wrote A Voice From the South; in it she passionately addressed the advancement and education of Black women in the United States:

> Let our girls feel that we expect something more of them than that they merely look pretty and appear well in society. Teach them that there is a race with special needs which they and only they can help; that the world needs and is already asking for their trained, efficient forces. Finally, if there is an ambitious girl with pluck and brain to take the higher education, encourage her to make the most of it. Let there be the same flourish of trumpets and clapping of hands as when a boy announces his determination to enter the lists.... Let her know that your heart is following her, that your hand, though she sees it not, is ready to support her.

The success of the book propelled Cooper to prominence. Women's groups and other organizations requested she speak before them; she was an articulate and self-assured speaker who always advocated the dignity and self-reliance of the Black woman. Her message, though perhaps focused on the Black woman, resonated with women of all races.

In 1893 she was one of only six Black women—Frances Harper among them—invited to address the World's Congress of Representative Women in Chicago. Her speech on "The Intellectual Progress of Colored Women of the United States since Emancipation" addressed education, but it also spoke of how the Black woman fit into the women's rights movement. "We take our stand on the solidarity of humanity, the oneness of life, and the unnaturalness and injustice of all special favoritisms, whether of sex, race, country, or condition," she intoned. Former Black abolitionist Frederick Douglass listened to her words and was so moved by them that he rose to publicly congratulate her and to express the pride he felt in how far Black women had come in their struggle for civil and educational rights in the 30 years since emancipation.

By the mid-1890s, Cooper had firmly established herself as a leader in the Black intelligentsia. She frequently joined forces with such noted educators and activists as W. E. B. Du Bois, Fannie Barrier Williams, and Charlotte Forten Grimké to advance the Black cause. In 1900, Cooper and Du Bois formed part of a U.S. delegation to the first Pan-African Conference in London, England. She was one of two women invited to address the international gathering; she spoke on "The Negro Problem in America." While in England she served on a committee that drafted an appeal to Queen Victoria calling for the end of injustices directed at her Black subjects living under apartheid in South Africa.

While Cooper was furthering the Black woman's cause, she continued to devote herself to teaching—her first love. In 1902, she was named the first Black female principal of the M Street school. Through the years Cooper developed a classical studies curriculum—focusing on teaching subjects such as math, science, and Latin—that led her students to be among the best and the brightest in the country, to compete at the highest levels, especially in the Ivy League schools. In 1903 she invited W. E. B. Du Bois, her friend and fellow advocate for classical studies, to come speak at the school on the country's attempt

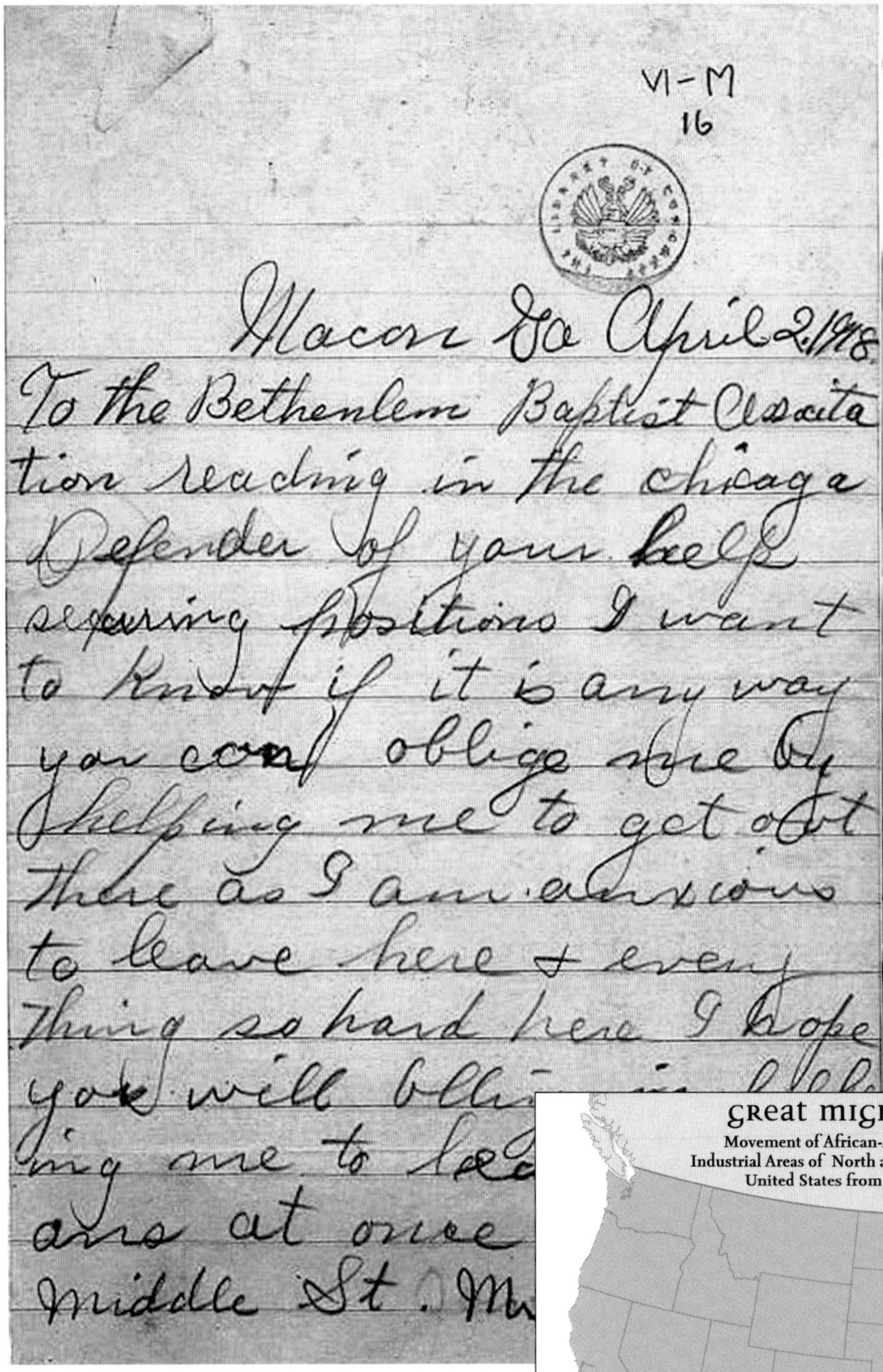

VI-M
16

Macon Ga April 2, 1918.
To the Bethenlem Baptist Asocia
tion reading in the chicaga
Defender of your help
securing positions I want
to know if it is any way
you can oblige me by
helping me to get out
there as I am anxious
to leave here + every
thing so hard here I hope
you will [oblige in] helping
[me to lea...]
ans at once
middle St. M...

19 FLORIDA 40
10-7126
PLEDGED TO
DRIVE SAFELY

GREAT MIGRATION
Movement of African-Americans to
Industrial Areas of North and North Central
United States from the South

CANADA

UNITED STATES

Detroit
Chicago
Cleveland
Boston
New York
Philadelphia
St. Louis

MEXICO

Black migrants from Florida take a rest on their way to New Jersey in the summer of 1940 for the potato harvest. Hard times at home and promises of a better life in the North compelled thousands of Black people to leave the South between 1915 and 1940 in what became known as the "Great Migration." Leaving by car was the exception rather than the rule; most migrant workers went by train, traveling the most direct route north to such cities as Chicago, Detroit, New York, and Philadelphia (see map). Many Southerners eager to leave wrote letters (far left) to Black churches and other charitable institutions seeking help in finding transportation, jobs, and housing.

to restrict the curriculum of colored schools. The popular education sentiment at that time was in favor of Booker T. Washington's industrial education. Many people thought Du Bois's Talented Tenth ideal was too elitist—the Washington, D.C., School Board included. Cooper's support for Du Bois and his philosophy made the Board of Education uneasy, and although its members valued Cooper's teaching experience, the Board decided against renewing Cooper's contract in 1904.

Cooper did not lack for teaching offers. She accepted the position of chair of languages at Lincoln University in Missouri. But in 1910, at the request of D.C.'s new superintendent of colored schools, she returned to the M Street school to teach Latin for the next 20 years. She continued advocating education as a means for social change. She continued her own love affair with education by taking graduate-level classes at Columbia University and other institutions, and in March 1925, at the age of 65, she earned a doctorate degree from the Sorbonne in Paris—making her the fourth African-American woman in history to earn a Ph.D. Only educators Georgiana R. Simpson and Eva B. Dykes and economist Sadie Tanner Mossell Alexander preceded her.

In 1930, Cooper was named the president of Frelinghuysen University, founded in Washington, D.C., by Jesse Lawson in 1907 to provide for the higher educational needs of "colored working people." In 1940 the university merged with other schools in Washington, D.C., and Cooper became its registrar. Always an educator, if only in spirit in later years, Cooper died at the age of 105 at her Washington, D.C., home in 1964. Her contributions to the Black community were profound as a social activist and educator.

Mary Eliza Church Terrell, Cooper's former classmate and colleague, also made a difference in the Black community. Her life differed from Cooper's in many ways. She was born in 1863 in Memphis, Tennessee, into a family of privilege. Her parents were slave-born of White men; however, following emancipation, they opened a saloon and a hair-dressing parlor; both ventures prospered and within a few years the Churches were among the wealthiest Black people in the United States. They divorced in 1869, but their commitment to their children never wavered.

Although Terrell enjoyed status in the Black community, her privileged background did not shield her from experiencing the racial prejudices of her time. While traveling with her father on a train, the conductor singled her out for removal from a coach that had been reserved for White people. Terrell was devastated. Her own father had passed as a White because of his light skin. After that, Terrell learned that her father and her grandparents had been slaves. The incident left a lasting impression on her.

"Do you know you have never lived until you have flown?" replied Bessie Coleman—America's first Black pilot—to a journalist who asked her why she "took up the game of flying." While working as a manicurist at a Chicago barbershop, Coleman became fascinated by the idea of flying. No American flight school would accept her, so she took French lessons, moved to France, and earned her license there (inset) in 1921. She was trained in parachuting and stunt flying, and performed for five years in the United States before dying doing what she loved.

She determined never to cower in the face of racism and to demonstrate the vast abilities of Black women. She believed that through education one gained the means to fight the social prejudices.

Terrell received a four-year bachelor's degree in the classics from Oberlin College in 1884. Afterward, she returned to Memphis to live with her father, but his disapproval of her desire to enter the working world stifled her. "I could not be happy leading a purposeless existence," she explained of her decision to find a teaching position. "All during my college course I had dreamed of the day when I could promote the welfare of my race." In 1885, she secured a position at Wilberforce College, where she taught a variety of subjects. Two years later she accepted a position at Washington, D. C.'s M Street High School, where she met her future husband, fellow teacher Robert Heberton Terrell.

She taught for only a year: She wished to broaden her horizons and visit other countries. Terrell was not willing just to accept the racial discrimination and Victorian ideals prevalent in the United States. She traveled for two years in Europe, experiencing new cultures, sharpening her language skills, and meeting influential people. All the while she witnessed and participated in a greater equality between races and between the sexes. She returned home resolved to advocate the same in the States.

Upon her return, Mary Church married Robert Terrell and retired from teaching. She remained involved with the women's clubs, keeping her hand in social reform. In 1892, her childhood friend Tom Moss was lynched in Memphis for no other reason than that his trading goods store was drawing customers away from White-owned businesses. Incensed, Terrell joined her friend Frederick Douglass in demanding a meeting with President Benjamin Harrison regarding the racial injustices and violence experienced by Black people. Harrison's apathy infuriated Mary Terrell. She realized that Black people would have to lead the way if change were to occur. She took up the banner with relish.

To carry out her convictions, Terrell attempted to join the White women's council of the National American Woman Suffrage Association. To her dismay, she met with resistance and was barred from membership. Unbowed, she became active in the Black Women's Club Movement, fighting for equal rights for Black women and for all civil rights. In 1892, she formed the Colored Women's League; in 1896, it merged with the Federation of Afro-American Women to become the National Association of Colored Women (NACW). She presided over the new organization as it developed programs to address racial problems through the elevation of Black women in employment and suffrage. The NACW took the lead in promoting social advantages for working mothers by establishing

The founding sisters of Delta Sigma Theta Sorority, some of whom are shown here, met at Howard University in 1913 to form a society not only of friendship but also of service. The women committed themselves to academic excellence on campus and community service off campus. Gwendolyn Boyd, the sorority's national president in 2003, spoke of the sorority's current members in terms reminiscent of the founders: "We're women who are about change. We feel compelled to make a difference. That's why we're Deltas."

kindergartens, day nurseries, and Mother Clubs. The Mother Clubs gave guidance on child rearing and household management; eventually the clubs took on other economic issues and raised funds to establish schools of domestic science—later called home economics. Within a decade the NACW had enhanced the lives of thousands of Black women and become the foremost Black women's group in the country, both politically and socially.

Terrell lobbied hard to integrate the Black and White suffrage movements. In 1901, thanks to her tireless campaigning, the NACW was invited to join the National Council of Women. Up to this point, there had been no significant Black presence in the suffrage movement, so their inclusion was a victory. Still, segregationist attitudes existed within the suffrage ranks: The Black women were expected to march behind the White women in a popular suffrage parade line in the summer of 1913. Terrell refused to accept the situation; her logic and persuasive speech to the organizers convinced them of its unfairness.

In 1901, Terrell started to advocate education as the means to enhance interracial cooperation: The more educated a Black woman was, the more she could compete with White people in a White-based society and prove her worth. Terrell traveled across the U.S., speaking out against segregation of any kind. Her passionate speeches drew admiring

crowds, who heard her message of reform. Terrell's popularity on the lecture circuit grew, and she found herself lecturing in front of White organizations as well. She was even invited to Berlin, Germany, in 1904 to speak at the International Council of Women, where she delivered her speech in fluent German.

Terrell's ideology about race relations and reform drew upon the ideals of Du Bois and Washington, but her strong leanings toward interracial cooperation were always paramount. She became ever more active in causes that she embraced. In 1909 she joined forces with Du Bois and White liberals to found the interracial NAACP, which from its inception accepted women members. It was established to advocate civil rights and suffrage for Black people. The NAACP chartered branches around the country; Terrell organized the Washington, D.C., branch in 1913.

Terrell's influence in the fight for equal rights for all Black people grew even stronger through the years. She proved herself a militant activist who wasn't afraid to picket, sit in, or boycott, depending on the situation. Her courage and unwavering commitment have inspired future generations of women. She died in 1954, at the age of 90, having lived long enough to witness the desegregation of public schools.

Another national figure who made tremendous strides as a leader in civil rights and education was Mary Jane McLeod Bethune. Bethune was born near Mayesville, South Carolina, in 1875. Her parents were diligent and prosperous farmers; they sent their daughter to a missionary school run by Emma J. Wilson. Here she received a "heart-in-hand" education that emphasized academic, religious, and vocational training. Wilson set an example for Bethune of what a well-educated Black woman could accomplish, inspiring Bethune to do the same.

In 1888, Bethune won a scholarship to the Scotia Seminary for Colored Girls in Concord, North Carolina, where she decided to dedicate herself to missionary work in Africa. Her dream was denied, however, because the Presbyterian order would not send African-American missionaries to Africa. Brokenhearted, but resolved to make a difference, she accepted a teaching position in 1895 at the Bible Institute for Home and Foreign Missions in Chicago.

The following year Bethune apprenticed at Lucy Craft Laney's Haines Institute in Augusta, Georgia, to learn its teaching methods. Students there were given a well-rounded

Three members of the Tattler Girls Athletic and Social Club—one of several girls' athletic clubs founded in the 1920s—prepare to take to the basketball court.

Opposite: Indianapolis school teacher Selma Beck made history in 1921 by founding the first Girl Scout troop for African Americans. Until then, the Girl Scouts had been for White people only.

Perched on the running board of her Chevrolet coupe in the summer of 1927, novelist and folklorist Zora Neale Hurston radiates joy. It was Hurston's celebration of being Black that made her an incomparable personality and mesmerizing voice of the Harlem Renaissance. "I do not belong to the sobbing school of Negrohood who hold that nature somehow gave them a lowdown dirty deal," she once wrote. "I have seen that the world is to the strong regardless of a little pigmentation more or less."

education—arts and sciences, music, sports—to prepare them to take on leadership roles in their communities. In addition, the institute instilled in its students the importance of raising families with strong moral Christian values. Bethune embraced the institute's teaching philosophy. In later years she would rely heavily on what she learned there, adding to it an emphasis on female-centered activism.

Following her year at the Haines Institute, Bethune spent a few years teaching in South Carolina, where she met and married Albertus Bethune, a clothing salesman. In 1903 they moved to Florida. Bethune decided to open her own school, since she felt the curriculum in the existing Black schools was too restrictive: In 1904 the Daytona Educational and Industrial School for Negro Girls opened its doors to five little girls—in a rented house and with a budget of $1.50.

Within six years the number of students had risen to 102 thanks to Bethune's tireless promotion and fundraising. The school's mission—as defined in its 1910 catalogue—was "to uplift Negro girls spiritually, morally, intellectually and industrially." The school's curriculum reflected Bethune's views of a practical education: basic academic subjects, homemaking, religious instruction, and industrial training. She encouraged her students to develop their creative urgings: "This in itself will do more to remove the walls of inter-racial prejudice and build up intra-racial confidence and pride than many of our educational tools and devices." Bethune invited Booker T. Washington to tour the school and see its benefits. His visit in 1912 brought the school national attention, further establishing its renown. In 1924 the school inaugurated a junior college curriculum. Five years later, the school merged with Cookman Institute, a boys school in Jacksonville, Florida, to become the four-year coeducational Bethune-Cookman College; Bethune served as the college's president.

Bethune's influence spread as she became very active in the Black Women's Club Movement. She stood out as a leader, motivating the women in their efforts and effecting change for Black people within society as a whole—from education to social reform.

Opposite: During the brutal economic crisis of the Great Depression, the Housewives' League of Detroit banded together for the first time in support of Black businesses and businesses that employed Black people. By choosing where to spend their money, Black housewives in Detroit and in similar leagues across the nation came to appreciate their own economic power. In the process, they helped secure jobs for thousands of Black workers and shocked many a White employer.

Two welders at work during World War II prove—as African-American women had been proving for all their lives—that women can do almost any job if put to the test. More than half the women who took jobs in America's wartime defense industry were housewives.

Her leadership qualities and her diplomatic skills interacting with the White community spread a positive image of the Black community. She founded many organizations, including the National Council of Negro Women, an umbrella organization that sought to foster communication, unity, and cooperation among Black women. Bethune envisioned it harnessing "the great power of nearly a million women into a force for constructive action."

She appealed to both Black and White audiences as a role model, earning her many opportunities to speak to various organizations on a vast array of platforms. In 1936, in a speech entitled "Closed Doors," Bethune exhorted that

> The principle of justice is fundamental and must be exercised if the peoples of this country are to rise to the highest and best, for there can be neither freedom, peace, true democracy or real development without justice. The closed door of economic inequalities, of educational limitation, of social restrictions comprise the greatest injustice possible. None need fear the change for which we plead. The door of opportunity with all its ramifications leading into every avenue can be opened without this evolution causing revolution. This is a high challenge to America—to the Church—and to the State....
>
> Awake America! Accept the challenge! Give the Negro a chance!

The message that Bethune spoke of and the passion with which she spoke drew the attention of President Franklin D. Roosevelt. In 1936, he named her to the Federal Council on Negro Affairs—the "Black Cabinet"—which was vested with promoting Black interests in his administration. She and her staff recruited more than a hundred Black managers and administrators for government positions during the Great Depression. She, herself, was appointed the Director of Negro Affairs for the National Youth Administration, making her the highest-ranking African-American woman in the government. She bore the informal title of "race leader at large." She opened doors beneficial to herself and others for many years to come, working diligently to improve the lives of all Black people.

Like Mary Church Terrell and countless others, Bethune picketed for integrated businesses and remained steadfast in her pursuit of equal rights for Black people. Bethune died in 1955 before the Civil Rights era, but she had laid the foundation for activists such as Coretta Scott King and Dorothy I. Height to pursue the goal of equality.

Rising from school teacher to presidential adviser, Mary McLeod Bethune (shown in her Washington, D.C., office in 1943) became one of the most powerful and effective Black women in America. "Most people think I am a dreamer," she once said. "Through dreams many things come true."

Following pages: Visions of strength and beauty, Delta sisters—among them Ruffenia Reese Carter (far left), the author's mother-in-law—gather on the steps of Dillard University in New Orleans in the late 1930s. They, like most alumni of Black sororities and fraternities, remained friends and community leaders long after graduation.

We must remake the world. The task is nothing less than that.

—Mary McLeod Bethune

6 speaking out

I'm sick and tired of being sick and tired!

—Fannie Lou Hamer

the early to mid-1900s was a paradoxical time in the United States. America was in the grip of legalized racism. The 1896 "separate but equal" ruling in *Plessy v. Ferguson* and Jim Crowism—the system of laws and customs that enforced racial segregation and discrimination throughout the U.S., especially in the South—dominated society. Yet more and more often, people challenged the laws as they started to come to terms with the changing economies and societies that followed World War I.

In 1960 a college student in pickets a diner in Reidsville, Georgia, that would not serve Black customers unless they remained standing. Such rules existed solely to reinforce the notion of White superiority.

Preceding pages: With 16 miles behind them and 34 to go, Civil Rights activists march from Selma to Montgomery in March of 1965 to petition for Black voting rights. Upon arrival, Martin Luther King, Jr., told supporters that they were on the move "like an idea whose time has come."

Chaos reigned in the cities during the "Red Summer of 1919," as Black people fought for equality. Racial tensions had been building following the end of World War I in part because Black people were moving north into once predominantly White areas, making White people uneasy, and Black soldiers, who had received equal treatment while fighting in Europe, were distressed to find their situations unimproved upon their return to the United States. At least 25 race riots occurred across the country in places such as Longview, Texas; Chicago, Illinois; Knoxville, Tennessee; Omaha, Nebraska; and Elaine, Arkansas. The rioting brought racism under public scrutiny, as did newspaper headlines when Black women were lynched. Between 1918 and 1927, 11 Black women were lynched, including 3 who were pregnant.

American attitudes were leaning toward desegregation, but change came slowly, and only through the dedicated activism of strong individuals. Black women—well-known or not—encountered conditions fostered by racism; however, they did not let racism stop them from leading rewarding lives. Nor did they let racism stop them from helping their people, and from speaking out in myriad ways through professional as well as social and civic means. One who became well-known was Marian Anderson.

Marian Anderson was born in 1902 in Philadelphia, Pennsylvania. She came from a loving, hardworking family of limited financial means. Anderson's talent was already apparent at the age of six, when she sang with the church choir. She loved singing more than anything. By the time she was ten she was featured on church handbills as the "baby contralto." All Anderson wanted was to study music. At South Philadelphia High School, the music teacher noticed Anderson's ability and invited her to sing with the school chorus. Her popularity grew as a singer—she performed at many events sponsored by church groups and her school.

As the years went by, Anderson felt the need for formal training. She took singing lessons from Black music teacher Mary Saunders Patterson, who gave Anderson a strong vocal foundation on which to build. Anderson tried to attend a formal music school, but she was humiliated when the school refused to give her an application because of her race. Her mother encouraged her never to give up on her dream. Since Patterson had taken Anderson as far as she could, Anderson auditioned for the renowned Giuseppe Boghetti. Impressed by her raw talent, he agreed to take her on as a student; however, the Andersons could not afford to pay for the lessons. Anderson's neighbors and fellow church members came to her support. They arranged a special gala concert to raise the money. The concert was a success and Anderson began her formal training. Under Boghetti's tutelage she learned songs in German, Italian, and French, developing a repertoire of more than 140 pieces.

Anderson got her first big break in 1925, when she won the opportunity to appear with the New York Philharmonic Orchestra. Her performance was a critical success. She spent the next several years studying and performing, mainly in Europe. It was not until the mid-1930s that Anderson's career began to rise in the United States.

By 1939, Anderson was known the world over. Yet she still met racial barriers. In 1939, her manager arranged for her to sing at Constitution Hall in Washington, D.C. Since it was the premier performance venue in the nation's capital, Anderson was thrilled—it meant she had truly "arrived." However, the Daughters of the American Revolution owned the property and refused to allow her to perform there. When First Lady Eleanor Roosevelt heard of the insult given to Anderson, she resigned her membership in protest. The news made national headlines. Anderson became a cause célèbre. After a series of conversations, Secretary of Interior Harold Ickes invited Anderson to perform a concert on Easter Sunday on the steps of the Lincoln Memorial. "In principle the idea was sound, but it could not be comfortable to me as an individual," she recounted later. "As I thought further, I could see that my significance as an individual was small in this affair. I had become, whether

Marian Anderson, whose exquisite voice became known around the world, sings on the steps of the Lincoln Memorial in 1952. Anderson enchanted a nation 13 years earlier from these same steps, when she sang at the invitation of Secretary of Interior Harold Ickes after having been barred from performing at Constitution Hall by the Daughters of the American Revolution because she was Black. On that day in 1939, it was her voice rather than her skin color that brought an audience of 75,000 to their feet in awe.

163

I liked it or not, a symbol, representing my people. I had to appear." The concert drew a crowd of 75,000 people. It was a momentous event for the artist as well as for the fledgling Civil Rights Movement. Anderson became a symbol of pride and possibility to hundreds of thousands of Black people.

Anderson's career was now a guaranteed success, but it was not until 16 years later that she realized a personal and professional dream: performing at the Metropolitan Opera in New York City, the premier opera venue in America. She played the role of Ulrica in Verdi's *Un Ballo in Maschera*. Anderson was the first African American invited to perform at the Met.

Anderson's achievements in the performing arts not only opened the doors for future Black artists, but they inspired all Black people, who saw in

A sheriff fingerprints Rosa Parks in February 1956, two months after she was arrested for refusing to give up her seat on a Montgomery bus to a White man. Her act of defiance triggered the year-long Montgomery bus boycott that ended on December 20, 1956, when the Supreme Court ruled segregation unlawful. The next day, Rosa Parks rode at the front of a bus (opposite). "People always say I didn't give up my seat because I was tired, but that isn't true," Parks later recalled. "No, the only tired I was, was tired of giving in."

them obvious signs of winning the struggle for equality. In appreciation of her contributions, President Jimmy Carter awarded Anderson the congressional Medal of Honor in 1977. She died in 1993.

Mattiwilda Dobbs grew up listening to Anderson and wishing to emulate her. Dobbs was born in 1925 in Atlanta, Georgia, into one of the South's most prestigious and political families. Her love affair with music began early in life: She started studying the piano and singing in the church choir when she was seven. Although all she wanted was to study music, Dobbs knew she needed to be prepared if she could not pursue a career as a singer. Like all five of her sisters, Dobbs attended Spelman College—the oldest Black women's college in the U.S. and a prestigious institute of higher education. She earned her B.A. in 1946 and followed it with an M.A. in Spanish language and literature from Columbia University Teachers College in 1948.

In 1947, Dobbs won the Marian Anderson Scholarship—a prize awarded to the most promising music student. This scholarship and the John Haw Whitney Fellowship she won a couple of years later made it possible for her to pursue her dream. She trained with noted voice teachers in the U.S. and abroad. Her talent propelled her to new heights in 1951 after she won the highly competitive International Music Competition in Geneva, Switzerland. Two years later, after proving herself at recitals, Dobbs finally got her big break.

In March 1953 Milan's famed La Scala invited Dobbs to perform Elvira in Rossini's *L'Italiana in Algeri*. She was the first Black person put under contract at La Scala and she performed night after night to a welcoming audience. The following month, Dobbs married Luis Rodriguez, a young Spaniard who had studied law at the Sorbonne. Their marriage was short-lived: Rodriguez took ill and died in June 1954. Only five days later, a grieving Dobbs summoned her strength to give a command performance for Queen Elizabeth II and the King and Queen of Sweden at Covent Garden. It was one of the greatest performances of her career; the King of Sweden was so

moved that he later honored her with his country's Order of the North Star.

Dobbs was now recognized worldwide as a premier opera singer; however, she still met discrimination and racism in the States. Segregation was very much a part of American life, especially in the South. Her hometown of Atlanta invited her to perform, but she refused to sing before a segregated audience. She would not compromise her values. Her attitude was that if some venues were not ready for her, others were: Her talent would overcome prejudices. In 1955 she broke the racial barrier at the San Francisco Opera. And in November 1956 she sang the role of Gilda in Verdi's *Rigoletto* at the Metropolitan Opera in New York City; she replaced Marian Anderson for the season. She went on to headline at venues across Europe and the United States, and even appeared on Ed Sullivan's television show, *Toast of the Town*. Her career soared; she made several recordings of operas and songs.

Dobbs retired from singing in the 1970s and turned her talents to training new generations of singers. Her last teaching position was in the late 1990s at Howard University, in Washington, D.C. Her professional accomplishments and her moral rectitude in the face of racial discrimination inspired legions of opera singers, music aficionados, and civil rights and political activists—including her nephew, the late Maynard H. Jackson, Atlanta's first Black mayor. Her influence continues today.

In 1940, one year after Marian Anderson's legendary performance on the steps of the Lincoln Memorial, 60 percent of all Black women in the labor force toiled in domestic service. Only 4.3 percent held professional, white-collar positions. This small but powerful group of women labored for the betterment of their families and other Black people's families. They used whatever professional, social, and civic means were available to them. They spoke out in myriad ways and came from all sectors of Black society.

Dorothy Celeste Boulding Ferebee was born in 1898 in Norfolk, Virginia. Although she came from a family of lawyers, she was always more interested in medicine than law: "In our family there was never a question of couldn't.... All my life I wanted to be a doctor. I would nurse and rub the birds that fell out of trees, the dog that lost a fight. My grandmother would say ... to my mother, 'she's going to make a fine doctor.' They weren't professional women but they gave me marvelous encouragement."

Dorothy earned her medical degree from Tufts University Medical School in Massachusetts in 1924 and immediately took a teaching position at Howard University Medical School, in Washington, D.C. She made it her life's mission to help "the poor, the old, the lonely, the young, the sick, the homeless and hungry, and the disabled." To that end, she set up a small practice in the poor section of Washington's Capital Hill neighborhood.

In 1935, the Alpha Kappa Alpha Sorority named Ferebee the medical director of its philanthropic Mississippi Health Project. Poverty-stricken Black people living in the Deep South had virtually no access to health care. Each summer, under Ferebee's direction, mobile field units traveled from small town to small town in rural counties, dispensing smallpox and diphtheria immunizations, teaching nutrition, and demonstrating proper hygiene. By the time Ferebee's tenure ended seven years later, some 15,000 people had been inoculated against diseases and countless more had received instructions in basic health care. Ferebee rose to national prominence in this position.

A few years later, in 1949, Ferebee was promoted to director of health services at Howard University, a position she would hold for 19 years; she also succeeded Mary McLeod Bethune as president of the National Council of Negro Women (NCNW). Ferebee guided the NCNW's fight for basic civil rights—equal voting standards, fair employment, and education. She encouraged the NCNW to become more active in fighting discrimination against

Under the watch of U.S. deputy marshals, six-year-old Ruby Bridges leaves William Frantz Elementary School in New Orleans in November 1960. After a federal court ordered the city to integrate its public schools, this little girl was the only Black child to enroll and break the color barrier. Angry White parents immediately withdrew their children in protest, not allowing them to return for many months. However, Ruby's classroom remained empty that entire year, save for Ruby and her teacher, neither of whom missed a day.

Black people in education, housing, and the armed forces. She led by example, taking her concerns to the highest in command. In a 1951 letter to President Harry S. Truman, Ferebee voiced that "the presence of the segregated Negro units belies the democratic principles" our government extols.

Ferebee excelled as a doctor and as a leader. In 1950, she was appointed to the Executive Committee for the White House Conference on Children and Youth. From the 1950s to the '70s, she sat on the boards of directors of the Young Women's Christian Association, ACTION (an outreach program for girls and women that provides assistance and shelter), and the Girl Scouts of the U.S.A. She was a member of President Kennedy's Council for Food for Peace and a medical consultant to the Peace Corps and the State Department.

Ferebee made an impact outside America as well. She was often invited to speak before international conferences, including the 1967 World Health Assembly in Geneva, Switzerland. In 1975, Ferebee headed the Washington, D.C., Metropolitan Area International Women's Year. Also in that year, she established the Women's Institute at American University in Washington, D.C.

CORETTA SCOTT KING AND MARTIN LUTHER KING, JR.,
CIVIL RIGHTS LEADERS, IN 1965

CORETTA SCOTT KING

Her tireless work for human rights is embodied in her epilogue for Barbara Reynolds's And Still We Rise.

From the time the first black people arrived, bound and shackled, in America in the year 1619...to today, the black experience has been characterized by slavery, segregation, and discrimination. Yet, somehow out of a terrible legacy of racism and suffering, a dynamic of faith and hope has steadily propelled black Americans forward in the quest for full human rights. Somehow we have survived the tearing apart of our families and the generation of poverty and brutality forced on us....Somehow, we have kept an unyielding belief in the promise of the American Dream.

Fresh from victory, sprinter Wilma Rudolph (above) displays the three gold medals that she won at the 1960 Olympics in Rome. She returned a heroine; however, she needed the protection of the National Guard (opposite) at a parade in her segregated Tennessee hometown. "When I was running," she said, "I had the sense of freedom, of running in the wind.... I felt like a butterfly." Her talent and grace inspired future generations of female athletes, Black and White.

Ferebee died in 1980. Her contributions to society stand testimony to her inspiring and unwavering commitment to the health and well-being of Black women.

Lawyer Sadie Tanner Mossell Alexander also worked tirelessly for the betterment of Black women. She was born in 1898 in Philadelphia, Pennsylvania. Both sides of her family were highly educated. Her father was a lawyer. Her grandfather, Benjamin Tucker Tanner, was the first editor of the A.M.E. *Church Review*, arguably the first African-American national journal. She had aunts and uncles who were artists, physicians, and scholars.

Following in their footsteps, Alexander attended the University of Pennsylvania. She excelled in her studies—taking only three years to earn her bachelor's degree in education, with honors. She later wrote about how in her freshman year she prayed every night for the strength to do her assignments to the best of her ability; she also prayed to learn to walk alone without being lonely since, initially, not one of her fellow women classmates—all White—would talk to her.

Drawing strength from her family's accomplishments and from within, Alexander pursued a doctorate in economics. When the University of Pennsylvania awarded her a Ph.D. in 1921, she was the second African-American woman to receive one in the

United States. While in school, Alexander joined the Delta Sigma Theta Sorority and served as its first national president from 1919 to 1923. The sorority gave Sadie a strong moral foundation on which she built her commitment to community service.

Although Alexander was an eminently qualified economist, she could not find work in Philadelphia in her field. She faced discrimination not only because she was Black, but because she was female. Frustrated, she moved to Durham, North Carolina, to work as an actuary for the African-American–owned North Mutual Life Insurance Company. Two years later, Alexander returned to Philadelphia to marry her college sweetheart and recent Harvard Law School graduate, Ray Pace Alexander. Bored with housework and buoyed by her husband's support, Alexander returned to school to earn a law degree. She graduated from the University of Pennsylvania Law School in 1927—the first African-American woman to do so. She was also the first Black woman to pass the bar in Pennsylvania. Alexander joined her husband's practice, focusing on estate and family law.

Alexander was a successful lawyer; however, she derived the most personal satisfaction from her work as an activist. The discrimination and insult she faced when she

Three Black protesters in Birmingham, Alabama, hold hands and brace themselves against the searing force of a fire hose. In May 1963 the Birmingham police repeatedly and brutally assaulted Civil Rights demonstrators. On May 4 they unleashed dogs and fire hoses on protesters— some as young as six—for the third time in as many days. Television cameras there broadcasted the images around the world: Outraged viewers watched as dogs tore at flesh and hoses slammed protesters to the ground. The city soon began negotiating an end to segregation practices with Black leaders through a hastily dispatched White House intermediary.

tried to find work as an economist drove her to fight for integration in the workplace. To that end, she spearheaded the drive to convince the University of Pennsylvania to hire African-American faculty members. She wrote letters to the President, lobbying for the integration of the U.S. armed forces. Her intelligence, tenacity, and zeal led President Harry S. Truman to appoint her to the 1946 Commission to Study the Civil Rights of All Races and Faiths. In 1948, she joined the American Civil Liberties Union. Over the next three decades she actively participated in its fight to uphold constitutionally guaranteed individual rights.

Alexander remained a committed activist even as she grew older. In 1963, she was one of the first to join President John F. Kennedy's nonpartisan Lawyers' Committee for Civil Rights under the Law. The organization mobilizes the pro bono resources of the private bar to litigate and advocate for civil rights. In 1978, President Jimmy Carter appointed her to the White House Conference on Aging. In 1982, Alexander retired from private practice and civil rights activism at the age of 85 due to the onset of Alzheimer's. She died seven years later.

alexander did not crusade alone for civil rights. In the 1950s, Rosa Louise McCauley Parks unwittingly managed, in one courageous act of defiance, to do more for the Civil Rights Movement than any one person previously.

Descended from former slaves, Parks was born in 1913 to parents of modest means in Tuskegee, Alabama. She married Raymond Parks, a barber, in 1932, after attending the all-Black Alabama State College. Both felt strongly about Black civil rights. Parks and her husband volunteered their time and energy to the local chapter of the National Association for the Advancement of Colored People (NAACP). She served as a youth advisor in the 1930s and formally joined the NAACP in 1943. She helped mobilize a statewide voter registration drive and was elected secretary of the Montgomery chapter. Her steadfast commitment to civil rights would soon be tested.

In the mid-1950s, the Montgomery bus system required Black people to enter the bus at the front to pay the fare and then exit to reenter at the rear. Many would miss their ride after the bus took off before they could reboard. Black riders were also forced to defer to White passengers when there were no more seats left on the bus, even though they paid the same fare. This angered many Black people, but they did not have any recourse.

In March 1955, 15-year-old Claudette Colvin was forcibly removed from a bus and jailed after she refused to give up her seat. "I done paid my dime—I ain't got no right to

On April 4, 1963, 19-year-old Dorothy Bell waits at a Birmingham lunch counter for service that would never come. The sit-in movement that swept the South began in 1960 under the leadership of the Student Nonviolent Coordinating Committee. Brave protesters of all ages, most of whom remained determinedly nonviolent, faced violence and abuse but ultimately succeeded in speeding the integration of public places in the South. While some restaurants chose to go out of business rather than change their policies, others eventually took down the "Whites Only" and "Colored Only" signs.

move," Colvin exclaimed. News of the incident spread, and a delegation of Civil Rights activists—including a young Black man named Martin Luther King, Jr.—arrived in Montgomery to support the local NAACP chapter in its call for justice for Colvin. Parks accompanied the delegation when it unsuccessfully asked the city to modify the seating policy. Nine months later, Parks experienced a situation similar to Colvin's.

The date was December 1, 1955. Parks was returning from the Montgomery Fair Department Store, where she worked as a tailor's assistant. She was sitting in the front row of the Colored section of the bus. A White man, finding no seats available in the Whites-only section, demanded she move. Parks refused, recalling later that "When I made that decision, I knew I had the strength of my ancestors with me." Like Colvin, she was arrested.

On the basis of the facts, the NAACP saw Parks's case as the perfect test case to challenge *Plessy v. Ferguson*. The NAACP was optimistic, since only a year earlier the Supreme

Court had ruled in *Brown v. Board of Education* that federally sanctioned "separate educational facilities are inherently unequal." The Women's Political Council (WPC), led by Jo Ann Robinson—a professor at Alabama State College who had suffered the same humiliation as Parks—suggested the idea of a one-day bus boycott. After Robinson had been arrested, she wrote the mayor of Montgomery a letter of protest. In it she had pointed out that Black people made up three-fifths of the bus ridership. Within a day, the WPC distributed more than 52,000 fliers announcing the boycott for December 5, the day of Parks's trial.

On December 5, 1955, the buses rolling through the streets of Montgomery were nearly empty as Black people by the thousands found alternate means of transportation. When Parks lost her case—she was fined $14, which she refused to pay—the NAACP took her case to the U.S. District Court. In support, the boycott continued until that court ruled in favor of the plaintiff. All told, 42,000 Black people walked, biked, taxied, or drove for a total of 381 days.

The overturning of *Plessy v. Ferguson* was a decisive turning point in the Civil Rights Movement, but it came with a personal cost. Parks was fired because of her involvement with the boycott and was unable to find another job in Montgomery. In 1957, she and her husband moved to Detroit, Michigan, in search of a better life. Despite her financial struggles, Parks remained committed to the fight for civil rights—and not just for African Americans: In the 1980s, she supported the South Africa antiapartheid movement. In the late 1990s, President Bill Clinton awarded Parks the two highest honors the nation can bestow on a civilian: the Presidential Medal of Freedom and the congressional Medal of Honor. The medals are tokens of the nation's gratitude and appreciation for Parks's distinguished contributions to society. Parks's seminal stand for justice and equality, her unflagging spirit and courage, and her unwavering commitment to civil rights earned her the name "Mother of the Civil Rights Movement."

In her fight for civil rights, Parks drew her courage, strength, and commitment from other Black women. Septima Poinsette Clark was one of them. Clark was born in Charleston, South Carolina, in 1898. Her parents instilled in her a strong commitment to society and education. After she had finished the public schooling available to Black people—through eighth grade—her parents sent her to the private Avery Normal Institute, a college and teachers preparatory school. She graduated in 1916. Clark had a love and aptitude for learning and wished to go to college, but her family could not afford the expense. Instead, she turned to teaching.

Clark found a position at the one-room Promised-Land School on St. John's Island, one of South Carolina's Sea Islands. She was one of only two teachers for the island children. Several adults, however, also approached Clark with the request she teach them to read and write. Intrigued by the idea, she passionately threw herself into the project, tutoring them individually and in small groups. Fighting adult illiteracy became her lifelong interest. In 1918, the Avery institute lured Clark back to Charleston, where she had her first taste of activism. She joined a group of women who were actively fighting to overturn the law disallowing Black people to teach in public schools. She went door to door persuasively arguing with people to sign a petition. Thanks to her help, the law was changed.

In 1919, she married Nerie Clark, a sailor she met in Charleston, and began to pursue her dream of a college education. She took summer classes and taught the rest of the year. When Nerie Clark's death in 1925 left her a widow, she returned to teach on St. John's Island; four years later she moved to Columbia, South Carolina, to take a better teaching position. She still took college classes during the summers. She finally received her bachelor's degree in 1942, after working toward it for more than 20 years; it took her four more years to earn her master's degree from Hampton Institute (now Hampton University), in Virginia.

In Columbia, Clark became an active member of the NAACP. She worked alongside lawyer Thurgood Marshall on a court case that successfully challenged the inequitable teaching salaries between Black and White people. She also ran night-school classes for adults. In 1956, on the heels of the *Brown v. Board of Education* ruling, South Carolina passed a law that forbade public school teachers from belonging to civil rights groups. Clark chose to acknowledge her proud association with the NAACP—and subsequently lost her job.

She didn't lack for offers though. She accepted the position of director of workshops at the Highlander Folk School in Chattanooga, Tennessee. The interracial institute was a training camp for community activists from all over the country. Eleanor Roosevelt, Martin Luther King, Jr., and Rosa Parks all participated in a workshop at one time, either as an attendee or as a speaker. The workshops emphasized the importance of voter education, civil rights, and social organization. Out of this, Clark came up with the idea of training people to teach at a new kind of school: a citizenship school. Clark envisioned the school as a place where illiterate adults could learn the basic skills every citizen of the United States needs to fully enjoy his or her constitutional rights.

The students would first learn to read and write—for if you could not read and write, you could not register to vote. Then they would focus on how to fill out voter

registration applications and other documents; how to manage money and write checks; how to understand the Social Security program; and much more. She opened the first citizenship school on St. John's Island in 1957. The school was a resounding success. And so was Clark's program. By 1966, the program had trained more than 10,000 teachers and established more than 800 citizenship schools. The schools turned out more than 70,000 African-American registered voters—one of the most pivotal components in the Civil Rights Movement.

Many of the newly registered voters were women—a fact that heartened Clark. She believed that "the work the women did during the time of civil rights is what really carried the movement along. The women carried forth the ideas. I think the civil rights movement would never have taken off if some women hadn't started to speak up."

Her dedication to the cause and the example she set influenced many men and women of the movement, including such notables as Andrew Young, John Lewis, and Hosea Williams. And although she retired in 1970 from active work with the Southern Christian Leadership Conference, where she had served since the age of 63 as director of education and training, Clark remained committed to social reform until the day she died in December 1987.

Clark's teachings had a profound impact on Fannie Lou Townsend Hamer. Born to sharecroppers in 1917 in Montgomery County, Mississippi, Hamer had only a few years of schooling before she began working full-time in the fields to help support her family. She married Percy Hamer, a sharecropper, at age 27 and moved to Sunflower County, Mississippi. There she worked for meager wages as a timekeeper and keeper of cotton weights on a cotton plantation. Her years were filled with the strain and sweat of plantation work in the South.

When she was 45 years old, she attended a meeting held by the Student Nonviolent Coordinating Committee (SNCC), a civil rights group that was encouraging Black people to register to vote in order to make a difference in their lives. Members of the committee explained how the state government was using illegal literacy tests, violent acts, poll taxes, and other means to deny Black people their constitutional right to vote. Hamer was incensed. In August 1962, she walked out of a cotton field and went to register to vote in Indianola, Mississippi. She failed the literacy test on the state constitution. Resolved to be able to register and to cast her vote, Hamer returned every 30 days to take the test again. She eventually passed the test in 1963.

Following Hamer's first attempt to register, her boss threatened to fire her if she tried again. Unafraid, she returned to take the test. "They set me free. It's the best thing that could happen. Now I can work for my people," Hamer said. Inspired by the SNCC's efforts to challenge racial and economic inequalities, she signed on as an SNCC fieldworker to get the message out about voter education and registration.

"I'm sick and tired of being sick and tired!" Hamer's powerful voice captivated crowds at rallies and meetings—when she spoke and when she sang soulful traditional spirituals such as "This Little Light of Mine." In June 1963, state troopers arrested and physically abused Hamer and her companions when they tried to eat at a Whites-only restaurant in Winona, Mississippi. At the jail, the police ordered two Black prisoners to "beat her until they were tired." The assault damaged one of Hamer's eyes and kidneys, but it couldn't dissuade her from her campaign to encourage voter registration among African Americans so they would have a say in their government.

Opposite: At the behest of lawyer Marian Wright Edelman (second from right), Senator Robert Kennedy visited poor Black residents of the Mississippi Delta in 1967 to see firsthand how desperately they were living.

With spellbinding passion, Fannie Lou Hamer—a former cotton picker who helped force the racial integration of Mississippi's Democratic Party—rallies a crowd outside the Capitol in Washington, D.C., on September 17, 1965.

Contestants in the 1972 Miss Black America pageant line up on stage. In the eyes of their admirers, these young women embodied the essence of "Black is Beautiful," a consciousness reflecting a new sense of racial pride that took hold in the late 1960s. To affirm their African roots, many people began to wear their hair in Afros, or Naturals, to dress in African-style clothing, adopt African names, participate in the Black Power movement. It would be 20 years before Vanessa L. Williams would be crowned the first Black winner of the Miss America pageant.

Hamer found the lack of Black voice in Congress disquieting. She strove to integrate Mississippi's Democratic Party. In 1964, she and a group of other activists founded the Mississippi Freedom Democratic Party (MFDP) to force the issue. She ran for Congress on the MFDP ticket and made national headlines. She lost in the primary, but she succeeded in raising the public's awareness. When the 1964 Democratic National Convention refused to give seats to MFDP delegates, Hamer went on television to deplore America's racial inequality. Hamer's activism contributed in no small part to the passage of the 1965 Voting Rights Act, which guaranteed Black people the right to vote. And in 1968, the newly integrated Democratic Party in Mississippi named Hamer a delegate to the 1968 Democratic National Convention. Hamer stayed involved in civil rights and issues of social welfare until her death in 1977.

Hamer was not alone in her struggle to gain equal treatment for her people. Dorothy I. Height has been at the vanguard of important issues relating to human, civil, family, and women's rights for more than 75 years. She was born in Richmond, Virginia,

A clenched fist symbolized Black Power, a new racial consciousness that took hold among African Americans in the late 1960s. Black Power was at once a declaration of self-reliance, a celebration of Blackness, and a call to revolutionary struggle against institutional racism.

Opposite: Angela Davis, whose name became forever linked to the "new generation" of Black activists, addresses a crowd of supporters. Professor, philosopher, and Black Panther, she began speaking out against social injustice in 1970 and has never stopped.

in 1912, into a large, loving family. Her family soon moved to Rankin, Pennsylvania—taking part in the migration of Black people leaving the South looking for more opportunities in the North.

A quick study, Height graduated in four years from New York University with both a bachelor's and a master's degree in educational psychology. She went on to do social work with the Young Women's Christian Association (YWCA). She quickly rose through the ranks to become the assistant director of the Harlem YWCA office. In that role, on November 7, 1937, Height escorted First Lady Eleanor Roosevelt into a meeting of the National Council of Negro Women (NCNW) that was held at the Harlem YWCA. Height's poise caught the attention of Mary McLeod Bethune, the NCNW's founder and president. She sought Height out afterward and asked her to join the council's fight for women's concerns. Height eagerly agreed and began volunteering for the NCNW.

From the 1930s to the late 1970s, Height was committed to social and progressive activism, often heading up many organizations at the same time. She was involved with

the Emma Ransom House, the Phyllis Wheatley Branch of the YWCA, and the National Board of the YWCA of the U.S.A. She served as national president of Delta Sigma Theta Sorority from 1947 to 1956 and as the director of the Center for Racial Justice from 1965 to 1977. In 1957, she assumed the role of leader of the NCNW, which she held until 1998.

As president of the NCNW, Height worked closely with Dr. Martin Luther King, Jr., Roy Wilkins, Whitney Young, A. Philip Randolph, and many others during the Civil Rights era, championing the rights of women and children. She actively participated in nearly all of the major events that were related to civil rights and human rights—including the 1963 March on Washington, where Height was one of only a few women on the platform with Dr. King as he delivered his famous "I Have a Dream" speech.

Height has followed in the footsteps of her mentor, Mary McLeod Bethune, by "harnessing the womanpower." Height has been praised as a masterful collaborator and coalition-builder. Her work and studies have taken her to countries in Africa, the Caribbean, Asia, and Europe, where she forged bonds with groups to realize a stronger voice in women's concerns. Under her leadership, the NCNW continued to grow as a strong coalition of women's organizations. Some of the greatest outcomes of her work are evidenced by the improvement in the lives of the families that have been helped by the NCNW. Among her many accomplishments, she sponsored voter registration drives and developed programs that addressed teenage parenting and hunger in rural areas.

Height's contributions to society have been noticed and rewarded by every United States President since Ronald Reagan, who awarded her the Citizens Medal Award for distinguished service in 1989. President Clinton awarded her the nation's highest civilian honor, the Presidential Medal of Freedom. In 2003, as president emerita and chair of the NCNW, Height has continued to work every day and travel extensively, even though she is in her 90s. Dorothy Height sets an example that can be successfully followed, even by women who are just beginning their careers. ♀

Mary Church Terrell, a life-long civil rights activist and a leader in the Black Women's Club Movement, stands in line at a recently integrated movie theater in Washington, D.C. In 1953, at age 90, she successfully led a movement to integrate public facilities in the nation's capital.

Following pages: A passenger riding a Dallas bus on April 24, 1956, points triumphantly to a "Blacks-to-the-back-of-the-bus" sign that would soon come down in response to the Supreme Court's decision to ban segregation on all forms of state public transportation.

NOTICE

IT IS REQUIRED BY LAW UNDER
PENALTY OF FINE OF $5.00 TO $25.00
THAT WHITE AND NEGRO PASSENGERS MUST
OCCUPY THE RESPECTIVE SPACE OR SEATS
INDICATED BY SIGNS IN THIS VEHICLE

TEXAS PENAL CODE ARTICLE 1659 SEC 4
DALLAS CITY ORDINANCE NO. 2904

If Rosa Parks had taken
a poll before she sat down
in the bus in Montgomery,
she'd still be standing.

—Mary Frances Berry

7 Leaders on the world stage

I do not weep at the world—I am too busy sharpening my oyster knife.

—Zora Neale Hurston

MS. JORDAN

a s the Civil Rights Movement came to prominence in the 1950s and '60s, the lives of Black people changed substantially. Even so, change did not come easily. Many leaders of the Civil Rights Movement and everyday citizens paid for the change with their lives. In 1968, Dr. Martin Luther King, Jr., was assassinated. For more than a decade he had led African Americans in Civil Rights campaigns and peaceful demonstrations, making a difference in social progress for people of all color. Left in his wake was a stunned following of Civil Rights devotees and a young family to mourn his loss. When tragedy struck, Coretta Scott King became a widow at age 40. This was not her first encounter with tragedy, nor was it the first time that she would exhibit strong leadership.

Coretta Scott King was born in 1927 in Marion, Alabama. She grew up on her grand-father's prosperous farm. Her father purchased a sawmill, and with his three trucks he hauled lumber from the sawmill. After two weeks and one payday, the sawmill was burned to ashes. Because of the climate of racial hatred and the segregationist way of life existing at the time, no one was ever brought to justice. The Scotts instilled in their children the value of a good education as a tool in the fight for civil rights. Coretta Scott King graduated from the semi-private Lincoln High School, which had an integrated faculty. She later attended Antioch College in Ohio and majored in elementary education and music. As in Alabama, she faced

Barbara Jordan, addressing fellow members of the House Judiciary Committee in 1974, followed her own counsel throughout an impressive political career. "If you are dissatisfied with the way things are," she said, "then you have got to resolve to change them." This she did, as a Texas senator and then as a three-term congresswoman.

Preceding pages: Carol Moseley-Braun cheers her supporters during her 1992 campaign for the U.S. Senate. She became the first African-American woman to serve in that body. In 2003, she began a bid for the highest office in the United States: the Presidency.

Coretta Scott King plays tenderly with her youngest child, Bernice, on an Atlanta sidewalk in November 1964. From the start, Coretta Scott King embraced the Civil Rights struggle as one for which she was destined. "I remember thinking one day in Montgomery [in 1956], 'This is what I have been preparing for my entire life. This is the beginning of a journey.'" Since her husband's death in 1968, she has become an internationally recognized voice for human rights.

PRESS BOX DEMOCRATIC PREFERENCE POLL

RESULTS
THROUGH WEEK OF
4 20

LINDSAY
HUMPHREY
McGOVERN
MUSKIE
WALLACE
CHISHOLM
OTHERS
TOTAL VOTES

JOHN V. LINDSAY   HUBERT H. HUMPHREY   GEORGE MC GOVERN

EDMUND S. MUSKIE   GEORGE WALLACE   SHIRLEY CHISHOLM

discrimination in Ohio. She sought to make a difference by joining the campus chapter of the National Association for the Advancement of Colored People (NAACP), a civil liberties committee, and a race relations committee.

Following her graduation, Coretta Scott King realized her true calling was music. She enrolled in Boston's New England Conservatory of Music. In Boston, she met Martin Luther King, Jr., who was completing his doctorate degree at Boston University. The couple married in 1953 and soon moved to Montgomery, Alabama, where Dr. King had secured a position as pastor at the Dexter Avenue Baptist Church. In 1960, the family moved to Atlanta, Georgia, where Dr. King was co-pastor of the Ebenezer Baptist Church; there Coretta Scott King taught voice lessons at Morris Brown College.

Dr. King rose to prominence in the Civil Rights Movement in the mid-1950s during the Montgomery bus boycott sparked by Rosa Parks's refusal to move from her bus seat. He was a gifted public speaker whose message of nonviolent protest resonated with

Black and White people. Support for Dr. King and the Civil Rights Movement grew—reaching a high on August 28, 1963, with the peaceful March on Washington. More than 200,000 people descended upon the capital to show their support for the Civil Rights cause. While many Civil Rights leaders spoke that day, it was Dr. King's "I Have a Dream" speech that riveted the nation. Standing on the steps of the Lincoln Memorial, in the shadow of the Great Emancipator, Dr. King spoke in ringing tones of his dream of one day seeing people of all colors and denominations standing side by side, free and equal.

Coretta Scott King's own passion and drive for equality still burned from her college years. In the early years of Dr. King's leadership, she performed classical music concerts, raised the couple's four children, and worked closely with her husband, planning marches and boycotts. As the children grew older, she moved to the forefront of the Civil Rights Movement. She and Dr. King traveled on civil and human rights missions throughout the world, including India, Africa, and Europe, sharing Dr. King's philosophy of nonviolence. Together they brought about a positive change in the Civil Rights struggle. In 1964, she performed in more than 30 "freedom concerts" of inspirational lectures, poetry, and songs that focused on civil rights to raise money for Dr. King's organization, the Southern Christian Leadership Conference.

In April 1968, Dr. King was killed by a sniper in Memphis, where he was mediating a strike. Coretta Scott King took up his torch with Andrew Young, Jesse Jackson, and others. She became a highly visible leader in the Civil Rights campaign. The peace rally on April 27 was her first speaking engagement. On Solidarity Day, June 19, 1968, she spoke to over 50,000 people on the Mall in Washington, D.C. It was the culmination of a series of events that Dr. King had set in motion to call attention to the plight of the nation's poor. The speech denoted her emergence as a Civil Rights leader. In it she called for women to "unite and form a solid block of women power" to fight against racism, poverty, and war.

In June 1968, Mrs. King founded the Atlanta-based Martin Luther King Memorial Center, which later became the Martin Luther King Center for Nonviolent Social Change. The Center's mission is to educate people on the Kingian philosophy in methods of non-violent social change. It is dedicated to spreading Dr. King's message of non-violence as a means to combat "high rates of child poverty, AIDS, the death penalty, domestic, community, and international violence, declining educational opportunities, and many forms of racism, bigotry, and discrimination." The next year Mrs. King published her first memoir, *My Life With Martin Luther King, Jr.*

Mrs. King took to heart the words of educator Horace Mann, learned in college:

Unforgettably cast among an all-White, all-male field—as this poster on display at a Miami polling station illustrated—Congresswoman Shirley Chisholm broke new ground when she campaigned for the Presidency of the United States in 1972. She ran as a "candidate of the people." She expected that her candidacy would draw national attention to the issues that concerned her and pave the way for others who could then "feel themselves as capable of running for high political office as any wealthy, good-looking white male."

"Be ashamed to die until you have won some victory for humanity." She has said: "I guess these words have haunted me all of my life." Mrs. King continues to deliver speeches on civil and human rights worldwide and to campaign for antiapartheidism, AIDS, and poverty.

Like her husband, she has never been afraid of being arrested for her beliefs—in 1983 she was jailed after protesting apartheid at the South African embassy in Washington, D.C.—because it only brought attention to the cause. She led the effort to establish her husband's birthday, January 15, as a federal holiday (the third Monday in January)—the first honoring an African American. Her commitment to social justice, urban renewal, and human rights touches people around the globe.

after several civil rights breakthroughs in the 1970s, many Black men found their voice in politics. Black women, however, had the additional obstacle of gender to overcome. Two women—Shirley Chisholm and Yvonne Brathwaite Burke—successfully overcame the barriers and made remarkable strides on the national political scene.

Shirley Chisholm was born Shirley Anita Saint Hill in 1924 in Brooklyn, New York. Her childhood was split between Brooklyn and Barbados, where her parents sent her to live with her grandmother for a number of years because they could barely make ends meet. Always an excellent student, Chisholm attended Brooklyn College, earning a bachelor's degree in sociology. After graduation, she taught at a nursery school in Harlem and attended evening classes at Columbia University; she obtained her master's degree in early childhood education in 1952. (In 1949, she married Jamaican-born Conrad Chisholm, a private investigator.) Her interest in children and their welfare drove Chisholm to volunteer for the Brooklyn chapter of the National Urban League—a community-based organization that sought to ensure civil rights, the education of children, and the self-sufficiency of adults—and the NAACP. As a volunteer, Chisholm participated in numerous debates that focused on minority rights.

Before long, Chisholm began to delve into politics, beginning with a local political organization, the 17th Assembly District Democratic Club. She and the other members successfully campaigned to elect a Black judge to the municipal court. Nevertheless, within the Democratic Party she observed how little power Black people had in general and the utter lack of power that Black women had in particular. Her confidence in the Democratic Club shaken, Chisholm joined other Black members of the club to form a new organization called the Unity Democratic Club, to help mobilize the Black and Hispanic vote. In 1964, Chisholm ran as its candidate for the New York State Assembly. After winning and

serving in that position for four years, she ran for the United States Congress in a bid to become the first African American to represent Brooklyn. Her campaign slogan: "Fighting Shirley Chisholm—Unbought and Unbossed." Winning the seat in a landslide, Chisholm became the first Black woman elected to the U.S. House of Representatives.

Chisholm's years of service were synonymous with her campaign slogan. She was a powerful charismatic speaker who could hold a crowd captive. Always a feisty woman, Chisholm left her mark in the arena of civil rights and women's issues during her 14 years in Congress. She fought for a higher minimum wage, federal aid for daycare facilities, and increased funding for schools. She supported equal rights for women, reintroducing the equal rights amendment in 1969. Thanks to her words and support, the amendment passed the House and Senate and was sent to the states for ratification:

Prejudice against blacks is becoming unacceptable although it will take years to eliminate it. But it is doomed because, slowly, white America is beginning to admit that it exists. Prejudice against women is still acceptable. There is very little understanding yet of the immorality involved in double pay scales and the classification of most of the better jobs as "for men only."... It is true that part of the problem has been that women have not been aggressive in demanding their rights. This was also true of the black population for many years. They submitted to oppression and even cooperated with it. Women have done the same thing.... Laws will not change

Affectionately known to students as "Sister President," Johnnetta Cole (opposite) became the first African-American woman president of Spelman College in 1988. She succeeded three White women and one Black man as leader of this more-than-a-century-old Black women's college in Atlanta that was founded as a school for freed female slaves. During Cole's presidency, Spelman ranked among the nation's top liberal arts colleges (banner, left), tripled its endowment, and launched community service and mentorship programs.

CALIFORNIA CONGRESSWOMAN YVONNE BRATHWAITE BURKE, IN 1988

YVONNE BRATHWAITE BURKE

One of the first African-American congresswomen,
she is on the Los Angeles Board of supervisors.
Here she shares the inspiration of her ancestry.

My grandfather was a Cherokee and he
talked a great deal about his grandmother,
who was very high in the tribe. So I grew
up believing that I had the ability to do
things. Everybody was very confident.
I think that all of our thinking in terms
of identification with people comes
from experiences that our ancestors had.
Sometimes young people say, "I don't
know if there are opportunities for Blacks
in this or for women in this." I say:
"Sit down and figure out what you would
like to do, whether you know anyone
who has done it or not. And try it."

such deep-seated problems overnight. But they can be used to provide protection for those who are most abused, and to begin the process of evolutionary change by compelling the insensitive majority to reexamine its unconscious attitudes.

Not content to stop at Congress, in 1972 Chisholm made the first African-American mainstream bid for the Presidency of the United States, attempting to gain the Democratic Party nomination. "I am not the candidate of Black America, although I am Black and proud," announced Chisholm. "I am not the candidate of the women's movement in this country, though I am a woman, and I am equally proud of that. I am not the candidate of any political bosses or special interests.... I am the candidate of the people." Her platform addressed the dual "disabilities" of race and gender. She spoke about the discrimination Black women face even within their own community. In 14 primaries she won about 3 percent of the vote. (To date, no woman—Democrat, Republican, or third party candidate—has even come close to surpassing this number.) Two key constituencies, women-led and Black-led organizations, did not support her. Unbowed, Chisholm returned to Congress, where she continued to fight for what she believed in.

In 1983 she retired and moved to upstate New York with her second husband. For the next two decades Chisholm remained politically active and involved with women's issues, fighting to end gender discrimination. In addition to teaching political science classes at various universities over the years, she helped found the National Political Congress for Black Women in 1984, and she was the keynote speaker for the National Women's Political Caucus in 1987. In 1993, President Clinton nominated Chisholm as ambassador to Jamaica, but the 69-year-old Chisholm declined due to poor health.

Yvonne Watson Brathwaite Burke blazed a formidable career in politics as well. Burke was born in 1932 in Los Angeles, California. Inspired and impressed by Loren Miller, who won the case that lifted restrictive covenants preventing Blacks from living in certain communities, Burke pursued a career in law. In 1956 she earned a law degree from the University of Southern California. She went into private practice in Los Angeles, but soon became active in state and local politics. She worked with notable and powerful people such as James Reese, one of the first Black people to be appointed a judge in Los Angeles, and Thomas Bradley, the first Black mayor of the city. She was also a member of the McCone Commission that was created to investigate the Los Angeles Watts riots of 1965. The study the commission released indicated that the riots stemmed from the community's increasing frustration and sense of marginalization by a largely White-run

Anita Hill prepares to testify before the Senate Judiciary Committee on October 11, 1991, during confirmation hearings of Clarence Thomas to the U.S. Supreme Court. As the nation and the world watched on television, Hill defended her allegations of sexual harassment against Judge Thomas, a previous boss. He adamantly denied the charges, and the committee chose to confirm him. Yet by "speaking truth to power," as she put it, Hill forced America to discuss sexual harassment and inspired a record number of women to seek political office in 1992.

The ever beautiful Tina Turner sets the crowd on fire at a 1996 concert in Paris. Born Annie Mae Bullock in Brownsville, Tennessee, in 1939, Tina's journey to fame began in an East St. Louis nightclub when she performed an impromptu number with the band. Only 17, she captivated the attention of guitarist Ike Turner, and they married. But their marriage and their stardom soured due to Ike's abuse of Tina. She says she found the strength in 1976 to leave him and the band through chanting Nam-myoho-renge-kyo from the Buddhist Lotus Sutra. In 1984 her stardom returned at age 44 with the release of Private Dancer. Befittingly for one of the greatest soul singers ever, she was inducted into the Rock and Roll Hall of Fame in 1991.

government. The schools in South Central Los Angeles—a predominantly Black neighborhood—were underfunded, the jobless rate was high, and the housing situations were substandard. The report clearly showed that the measures the state had taken to circumvent the Civil Rights Act of 1964 contributed to the rising racial tensions.

Afterward, she served six years in the California State Assembly. She worked to improve housing and urban development for low income families by helping to pass legislation regarding tenants' rights. She also fought for improved health care.

In 1972, Burke decided to run for Congress. She became the first Black woman elected—she defeated six White men—from California to serve in the U.S. House of Representatives. During her three terms in office she championed child care, low-income housing, and education. She sat on the powerful Committee on Appropriations, and in 1976 she became the first woman to chair the Congressional Black Caucus. Popular with her constituents and with the members of Congress, Burke's political career looked to be on the rise. However, in 1978, she resigned.

In 1973, she had given birth to a daughter, becoming the first Congresswoman to have a baby while serving. She juggled motherhood and a demanding professional schedule, traveling with her daughter back and forth to California. Her actions showed Congress that women could work and have a family, too. However, when her daughter reached school age, Burke chose to give her child a stable life. She returned to private practice in Los Angeles, only to reenter public service in 1992, when she was elected to the Los Angeles County Board of Supervisors.

As one of the first African-American females to win a seat in the United States Congress, Burke helped pave the way for future Black women to hold public office.

Nearly 20 years after California sent Yvonne Brathwaite Burke to Congress, the state sent Maxine Waters. Born and raised in St. Louis, Missouri, 23-year-old Waters moved to Los Angeles with her husband, Edward Waters, in 1961. She found work at a garment factory and at a telephone company. After the Watts riots of 1965, Waters took a job as an assistant teacher in the newly created Head Start program sponsored by the federal government. Head Start was meant to address the social, nutritional, health, and psychological needs of children from low-income families, but many parents were frustrated by the lack of control or input they had in the program. Waters taught the parents how to contact legislatures and agencies to demand that the program be tailored to fit the needs of their community. Her experience filled her with a desire to make a difference in people's lives. She enrolled in California State University in 1968 to study sociology; in the same year she divorced her husband, Edward. Still working at Head Start, she completed her bachelor's degree, graduating in 1972 after only three and a half years.

Through her community activism, Waters interacted with many politicians and businesspeople in Los Angeles. Her ability to mobilize and motivate people won her a post as chief deputy to city council member David Cunningham, from 1973 to 1976. Then, convinced she could do more for her community, Waters successfully ran for the California State Assembly in 1976; she served for 14 years. Waters demonstrated that she was not afraid to confront controversial issues. She tirelessly urged United States companies to stop doing business with the apartheid-based government in South Africa. To press the issue, she secured the passage of a landmark law that required California to divest state pension funds from firms doing business in South Africa. She spearheaded the passage of affirmative action legislation that guaranteed women- and minority-owned businesses access to state funding opportunities.

In 1990, Waters ran for the seat in California's 29th Congressional District. Even though her opponent was endorsed in the primary, Waters won 88 percent of the votes. Then, in the general election, she won a resounding 80 percent of the votes. She was reelected in 1992 and 1994 by even larger margins.

In 1992, Waters effectively handled the riots that occurred in her district following the Rodney King verdict. King's beating by four policemen had been televised across the country; its brutality outraged America. When the police were acquitted of any wrongdoing, Black people in South Central Los Angeles, where the beating occurred, rioted out of disbelief and frustration. In six days of rioting, 54 people were killed, about 2,400 people were injured, and more than 13,200 were arrested. The angry residents had torched and looted scores of businesses. Waters's Los Angeles office burned down in the rioting. In the wake of the riots she succeeded in appropriating three million dollars from the Community Development Block Grant program for rebuilding the neighborhood, and helped smooth relations between the community and the police. She earned the respect of thousands of people as she attempted to create new lives for her constituents.

Since taking office in Congress, Waters has proven herself on the Banking, Finance and Urban Affairs Committee; the Small Business Committee; and the Veterans' Affairs Committee. She has also successfully headed the Congressional Black Caucus. Waters has always had a proactive stance on issues she cares about: "Whether the issue is empowering

our youth or striking a blow against crime, improving the veterans' services or helping our small businesspeople, I believe in a hands-on approach to solving our community's problems. Creating jobs and promoting economic opportunities are my first priorities." In 2003, Waters continued to serve in Congress, remaining deeply committed to such issues as unemployment and human rights, which impact her constituents—and all people who are underserved on a national or international level, especially women, children, and minorities.

Waters's commitment to women's rights in the workplace was galvanized by the treatment of Anita Faye Hill during the Hill-Thomas hearings of 1991. Hill, a 35-year-old law professor from Oklahoma, made national and world headlines when she courageously spoke in public about the sexual harassment she had experienced earlier when working for Clarence Thomas, then a nominee to the U.S. Supreme Court. In the process, she inadvertently revolutionized sexual politics in the workplace.

In 1981 Hill, a recent graduate from Yale Law School, accepted a position as assistant to Clarence Thomas, an assistant secretary at the U.S. Department of Education. Their working relationship was good for a while, but Hill said she soon felt uncomfortable with Thomas's sexual overtures, indecent comments, and requests for dates. Hill continued to be Thomas's assistant when he took over the chair of the Equal Employment Opportunity Commission (EEOC), but in early 1983 she accepted a teaching position at the University of Oklahoma in order to escape the mounting pressure she felt from Thomas.

In the fall of 1991, President George Bush nominated Thomas for the U.S. Supreme Court seat vacated by retiring Justice Thurgood Marshall. In the course of Thomas's background check, the FBI talked with Hill. She provided a sworn and confidential statement detailing the sexual harassment she encountered working with Thomas. Somehow National Public Radio received a copy of her statement and broadcast her allegations. The Judiciary Committee convened a hearing to address Hill's allegations of misconduct. The proceedings were televised live to millions of Americans and an international audience. Hill related with dignity how Thomas had used explicit and coarse language in her presence, made references to sexual acts, and detailed his sexual preferences. Thomas steadfastly refuted her allegations. It was a classic case of "he said, she said," with Thomas calling the hearings an "electronic lynching." The majority of the committee members believed Thomas. The Senate later approved his confirmation in a vote of 52 to 48.

Yet, Hill had made her mark. Before her revelation, sexual harassment in the workplace was seldom discussed. Afterward, it became a highly sensitive concern, sparking a contentious dialogue that ran—and still does today—along political, gender, and racial lines. In a show of support, more than 1,500 Black women signed a statement entitled "African American Women in Defense of Ourselves" that ran in the *New York Times* on November 18, 1991. It voiced the women's objections to the Thomas appointment and to the conduct of the Hill-Thomas hearings.

Washington, D.C., Mayor Sharon Pratt Kelly and Civil Rights icon Jesse Jackson lead a 1993 rally for D.C. statehood (opposite). Moments later, Kelly is arrested along with other protesters (below). Coming into office in 1990 as the city's first Black female mayor, Kelly promised to clean up city politics, improve city services, and reduce crime. She soon found her efforts frustrated by what she perceived as the federal government's peculiar role in making city policy. Rather than accept the status quo, she began to champion the idea of full-fledged statehood for the District of Columbia.

An election official in Kenya helps an 80-year-old woman cast her vote for president at a rural polling station on December 27, 2002. All over the country, people came by foot, on bicycle, and crammed into minibuses to participate in the election of a successor to Daniel arap Moi, who had ruled Kenya with an iron fist and stunning neglect for more than two decades. Such images and stories from around the world often serve to remind young Americans of the power of the vote, whose true worth is understood only when it has been denied.

Hill's decision to come forward to reveal mistreatment in the workplace emboldened many women to do the same, prompting major advancements in women's rights in the workplace. Women's awareness of sexual harassment laws has been heightened, and women are less afraid and embarrassed to confront harassment—knowing that they now have recourse. Statistics issued by the EEOC show that sexual harassment cases more than doubled from 6,127 in 1991 to 15,342 in 1996. According to the *Chronicle of Higher Education*, the Senate hearings made Hill a national icon for the issue of sexual harassment. Following the hearings, Hill took a sabbatical from teaching at the University of Oklahoma to devote time to writing and speaking about sexual harassment to organizations nationwide, further championing women's rights in the workplace.

anger ran high among women of all races during the Hill-Thomas hearings. The outrageous treatment Hill received by the male-dominated Congress made them realize that women were grossly underrepresented in Congress. That following election year, 1992, more than 150 women ran for seats in the House and Senate—42 women were elected. Carol Moseley-Braun was one of them. She made history when she became the first African-American female senator. She was also the only African American in the Senate. The last Black senator to serve had been Edward W. Brooke of Massachusetts, elected in 1966.

Moseley-Braun was born in 1947 in Chicago, Illinois. She attended public schools and received her undergraduate degree at the University of Illinois at Chicago. After completing her law degree at the University of Chicago, she worked for three years as a prosecutor for the U.S. Attorney's office. In that position, she won the U.S. Attorney General's Special Achievement Award for her work in housing, environmental law, and health policy.

Raised to believe in government and good citizenship, Moseley-Braun saw it as her duty to fight for her beliefs. In 1978, she ran for and was elected to the Illinois House of Representatives, where she became the first Black person to serve as assistant majority leader. Moseley-Braun championed school funding bills, public school parent councils, and bills designed to ban discrimination in housing and in private clubs.

In 1988, she was part of Mayor Harold Washington's multiethnic and gender-balanced "Dream Team" ticket, and was elected as Cook County's recorder of deeds. She revolutionized the office's operations, making it an efficient and profitable bureau, saving thousands of tax dollars. Around this time, her supporters urged her to consider challenging

An American soldier lifts weights while camped in the Saudi Arabian desert in 1991 during the first Gulf War. Women now serve in every branch of the U.S. military, but the right to serve and fight was hard won. This was especially true for Black women, who had to overcome the dual obstacles of race and gender. Not until 1948, when President Harry S. Truman issued an executive order desegregating the armed forces, did women of every color begin to infiltrate the military ranks.

the two-term incumbent senator, Alan Dixon, who had supported Supreme Court nominee Clarence Thomas. Angered by the Hill-Thomas hearings, Moseley-Braun ran a positive campaign that emphasized her outstanding record and focused on the issues. Even though Dixon outspent her 20-to-1, Moseley-Braun upset him in the primary; she then defeated Republican Richard Williamson in the general election with 53 percent of the vote.

While in the Senate, Moseley-Braun battled for issues that benefited her constituents and others across the nation, ranging from minority rights to economic justice to education reform. She held a powerful post on the Senate Finance Committee, where she became well-known for her ability to build consensus and negotiate—invaluable skills in an environment catering to disparate interests. She remained a principled woman and fought tenaciously for what she believed in, unafraid to take on rivals. She squared off against Republican Senator Jesse Helms when he proposed to renew a patent featuring the

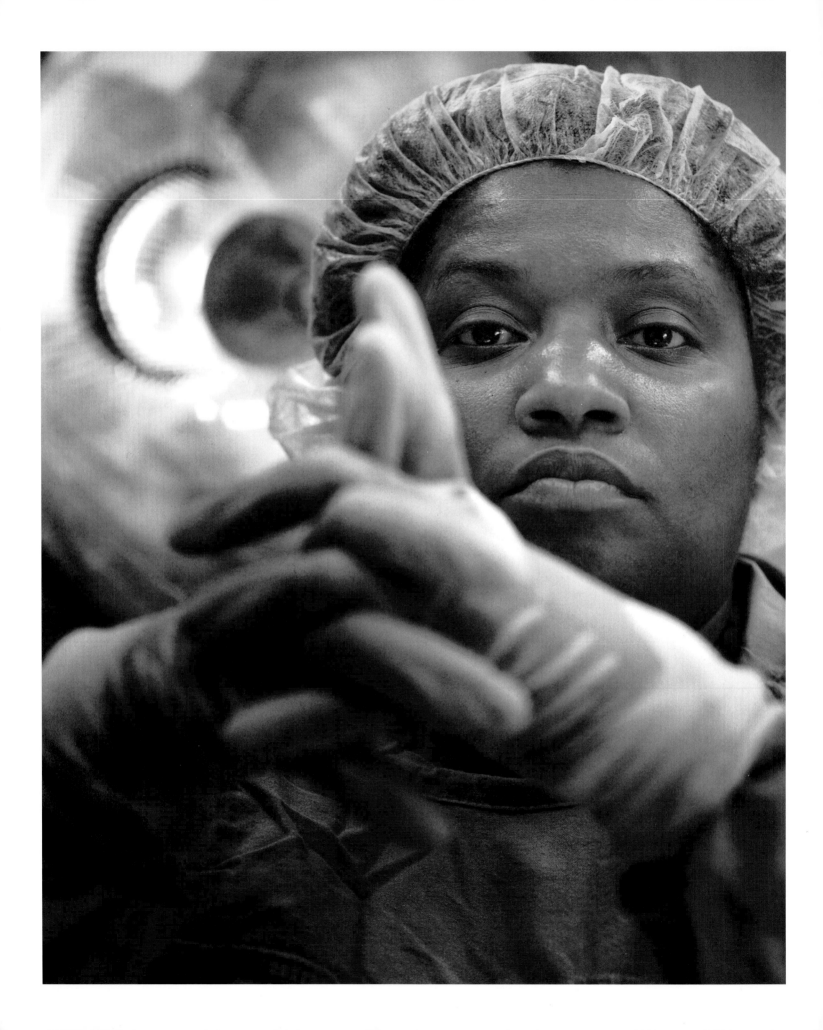

Confederate flag. Her passionate speech on the Senate floor—"There are those who would keep us slipping back into the darkness of division, into the snake pit of racial hatred, of racial antagonism and of support for symbols of the struggle to keep African Americans in bondage"—convinced the members to reverse their vote.

Moseley-Braun lost her reelection bid in 1998. Rumors of an improper association with Nigerian military dictator General Sani Abacha and allegations of financial misconduct surfaced, casting a pall on her campaign. But they were never proven. In 1999, President Bill Clinton appointed her ambassador to New Zealand. When the Bush Administration took office, Moseley-Braun returned to private life, teaching political science at Morris Brown College, in Atlanta. Never one to ignore duty to her gender, her race, and her country, she announced in 2003 that she was running for President of the United States in the 2004 election. "I have raised my voice to speak truth to power in public debate. And now I am prepared to breach the last barrier, shatter the last great glass ceiling that limits the contributions a woman can make in the leadership of this country."

Alexis Herman, another political appointee of President Bill Clinton, served as Secretary of Labor in his administration. Alexis Margaret Herman was born in 1947 in Mobile, Alabama. She received a bachelor of science degree in sociology in 1969 from Xavier University in New Orleans.

After college, Herman worked with the innovative Recruitment and Training Program in Pascagoula, Mississippi, that was designed to help unemployed Black people find apprenticeships in the building and construction trades. "I will never forget these young men," Herman said. "Their hearts—and their hands—were aching for the dignity of useful work. And as we offered them education, training, and information about jobs, many of them seized the opportunities placed before them." Impressed by the success of the program, the Southern Regional Council in Atlanta tapped Herman to develop a similar program to help Black women enter the white-collar workforce. The Minority Women Employment Program went national two years later with Herman at its helm. Hundreds of women of color participated in the program and were placed in white-collar and nontraditional jobs.

Herman took positions in her career that placed her in the forefront of community labor projects; her skills did not go unnoticed. She served four years in the Carter Administration as the director of the Department of Labor's Women's Bureau. At 29, she was the senior Black woman in the Labor Department and the youngest person ever to head the Women's Bureau. Herman advised the labor secretary and the President on women's concerns in the workplace, including rigid work schedules and child care.

In 1980 Alexa Canady became America's first Black neurosurgeon. She attributes her success not only to herself, but also to those who risked all during the Civil Rights Movement to secure Black people opportunity. "It's just as important for the White male to train with me as it is for the Black woman," she insists. "It's important for them both to know that neurosurgery is not the White man's province."

She specifically targeted ways to give women marketable job skills and the qualifications to succeed in nontraditional career fields. Herman saw affirmative action as a key to providing Black women with equal opportunities for education and training, to raise them up from domestic and industrial jobs.

Following her work with the Department of Labor, Herman founded and presided over the Washington, D.C.-based management firm A.M. Herman and Associates, advising corporations and state and local governments on human resources issues. She served a number of years with the Democratic National Committee, first as chief of staff and then as deputy chair. As the chief executive officer of the 1992 Democratic National Convention Committee, she gained high-level experience as the chief strategist in the management and production of the convention.

Herman's success led to her serving as the director of the White House Office of Public Liaison in the Clinton Administration, reporting directly to President Clinton and proving herself one of his staunchest advisors and allies throughout his Presidency. She served as his Secretary of Labor from May 1997 to January 2001. In 2000 she married physician Dr. Charles Franklin. She initiated many outreach programs: A Women's Customer Service Day educated workers about their benefits under the law; the Youth Opportunity Movement helped prepare inner-city youths to enter the workforce by providing them with training, education, and the skills to job search. In her final days as secretary, Herman summarized her department's—and her—accomplishments.

> Because of the 22.5 million jobs that we have created, because of our investments in education and training, unemployment is the lowest it has been in 30 years, and the lowest ever for African Americans and Latinos. With creativity and compassion we moved people from the welfare rolls to paychecks. We helped to make it possible for millions of women ... and men ... to take advantage of the Family and Medical Leave Act.

Herman's commitment to serving average working persons, and to bettering their workplaces and their lives, is gaining momentum as she builds on her firm foundation. ♀

Two dancers perform in Revelations, a production by the Alvin Ailey American Dance Theater. The company is under the direction of Judith Jamison, a premier dancer turned choreographer who has created several works that celebrate being a woman and being African American.

Following pages: With her husband President Nelson Mandela watching, Graça Machel releases a dove at The Hague during a South African state visit to the Netherlands in 1999. A leader in her own right, Machel has worked tirelessly to eliminate poverty in Africa and help women and children.

I have learned in the past decade of working with and listening to thousands of Black women from all walks of life that special kinds of power exist in our history.

—Darlene Clark Hine

8 setting the pace in the new millennium

Be mindful of the spiritual forces that gave us strength.
For it is in these struggles—reflections of the past—
that we derive a certain amount of strength, fortitude
and tenacity to boldly face the problems of today.

—Mona Bailey

across the world the new millennium brought the promise of a new era for millions of Black people who labored to move from the margins of society into the limelight. In the United States, the 1990s ushered in a Renaissance Noir, or a Black resurgence in education, politics, government, the arts, business, and popular culture. This rebirth began around the time that President-elect Bill Clinton asked author, professor, actress, director, and poet Maya Angelou to write and deliver a poem at his 1993 Inaugural ceremony. Her recitation of "On the Pulse of Morning" became an instant source of pride for Blacks the world over—and for Americans of all hues.

Maya Angelou was born Marguerite Johnson in 1928 in St. Louis, Missouri. After her parents divorced when she was three years old, Maya and her brother lived with their paternal grandmother, Annie Henderson, in Stamps, Arkansas. Henderson, a businesswoman who ran a small general store, was a strong role model for young Angelou. From her, Angelou learned common sense and the ability to control her own destiny. Henderson and the people of her church helped instill in Angelou a sense of belonging and she began to get a sense of a Black tradition.

When Angelou was eight years old, she visited her mother in St. Louis. Her mother's boyfriend raped her. He was convicted for his crime and jailed; shortly thereafter, he was found dead—apparently kicked to death. Already traumatized by the rape, Angelou believed that because she accused him of rape, she was responsible for his death. The psychologically

Halle Berry leaves the stage after making movie history as the first African-American woman to win a coveted Best Actress award at the Academy Awards in March 2002. "This moment," said an emotional Berry, "is for every nameless, faceless woman of color who now has a chance because this door tonight has been opened."

Preceding pages: A woman at a 1994 Afro-American Traditions festival in New York City beams with pride at a t-shirt advertising her smarts. For Black women as a whole, the modern combination of education and opportunity has been both liberating and empowering.

221

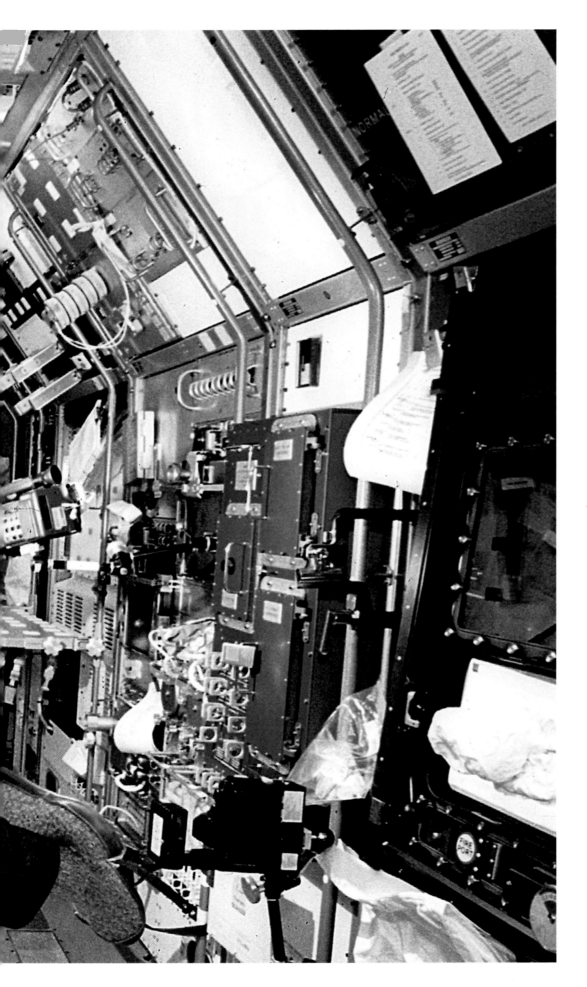

Dr. Mae Jemison, a mission specialist for NASA, floats in zero gravity aboard the space shuttle Endeavour in 1992. In this journey beyond Earth's realm, Jemison went where no other Black woman had gone before. Only four years earlier, she completed training and became the first African-American female astronaut in NASA history. She was one of only 15 accepted from 2,000 applicants to the program. She is now a professor, businesswoman, and founder of a math and science academy for young children. Jemison has said "I truly feel that someone interested in science is interested in understanding what's going on in the world."

scarred child turned mute. Her mother—frustrated and concerned—sent her back to her grandmother. Henderson's care had a soothing effect on Angelou, and after five long years Angelou spoke again. During that time, a neighbor tried to encourage Angelou to speak

by giving her books and poetry to read and recite. Angelou started writing for herself.

After Angelou graduated from eighth grade at the head of her class, she and her brother joined their mother in San Francisco. Life in the big city was more sophisticated than it had been in Stamps, Arkansas. Angelou ran wild, finding the streets of San Francisco a challenge by day and night. At 17, she gave birth to her son, Guy—described by Angelou as her greatest blessing. The next few years were dif-

ficult times for the teenage mother. She flirted with drugs and switched from one low-paying job to another with regularity—at one point she even pimped two lesbian prostitutes.

At 22, Angelou married a White former sailor named Tosh Angelos; at 24, she divorced him. Increasingly drawn to the arts, she studied dance and took up acting. She was good at it and was able to make a living as a professional stage artist. In the mid-1950s, she toured around Europe and Africa in a production company of the opera *Porgy and Bess*. The camaraderie and professionalism of the acting troupe and the story and spirituality of the play gave Angelou a sense of security. She began to come to terms with the events of her childhood and learned to take pride in herself as a strong Black woman.

On her return to the U.S., she moved to New York and dedicated herself to making Black people think about themselves, their society, their place in the world. She expressed herself in poems and short stories. In 1960 she heard Dr. Martin Luther King, Jr., talk. Inspired, she co-wrote a musical revue, *Cabaret for Freedom*, to benefit King's Southern Christian Leadership Conference (SCLC). King asked Angelou to work as a coordinator for the nascent SCLC. After a short period working with people to end racial discrimination in America, Angelou decided to explore her roots in a journey to Africa. Over the next few years Angelou lived in Egypt and Ghana, supporting herself as a journalist and teacher. She returned to the United States in 1966.

Resolved to exorcise her childhood demons, Angelou authored the autobiographical I know Why The Caged Bird Sings, published in 1971. It soon became a best-seller as, across the nation, Africana women—and women in general—bought the book and found themselves in it. Angelou went on to write a series of autobiographical works, each a lament and a tribute to her past. Angelou offered strong images of Black women in her stories and poetry at a time when Black women were sorely underrepresented in literature. "We need to see our mothers, aunts, our sisters, and grandmothers," said Angelou. She felt a responsibility to provide these images for Black women. "Phenomenal Woman" (1978) and "Still I Rise" (1979)—her two most important poems that celebrate Black women—extol the strength, pride, and beauty of the Africana woman, demanding that people realize the woman of African heritage is a force to be reckoned with.

In 1971, she was nominated for the Pulitzer Prize in poetry for the collection Just Give Me a Cool Drink of Water 'fore I Diiie. In 1981, she accepted a lifetime appointment as the Reynolds Professor in American Studies at Wake Forest University in North Carolina.

Angelou has received many honors for her outstanding achievements and service to the African-American community, including the NAACP Spingarn Medal—the highest honor the organization bestows—and the NCNW Uncommon Height Award. Her works offer readers a glimpse of Angelou's passion and strength of character. They inspire legions of Black women, giving them hope and self-respect.

Growing up at the same time as Maya Angelou was a young aspiring novelist who one day would be called Toni Morrison. As one of the most important writers in the history of this nation—and in the world—Morrison has won both a Pulitzer Prize (1988) for her novel, Beloved, and a Nobel Prize for literature (1993) for her body of work, making her the first African American to do so.

Born Chloe Anthony Wofford in Lorain, Ohio, in 1931, Morrison loved books and was a voracious reader. After graduating with honors from high school, she attended Howard University, graduating in 1953 with a bachelor's degree in English. She continued her education at Cornell University, earning a master's degree in English literature in 1955.

She returned to Howard University to teach English in 1957. There she met and married Jamaican architect Harold Morrison. While at Howard, Toni Morrison started

Poet Maya Angelou turns to hug newly sworn-in President Bill Clinton after reciting her poem, "On the Pulse of Morning," at his Inauguration ceremony in Washington, D.C., on January 20, 1993. The beautiful words that she spoke that morning on the west steps of the Capitol challenged her nation with a message of remembrance, humility, and hope.

Toni Morrison, one of the
world's most celebrated
writers, enjoys an evening in
her honor in New York City
in 1994. Morrison has an
incomparable gift with
language that makes poetry
of prose. She writes stories of
Black women—"women who
were silenced"—set in the
Black community, but she
can be categorized as neither
a "women's writer" nor an
"African-American writer."
Her novels have a universal
appeal; they are read and
appreciated worldwide.

writing short stories, more for her own personal pleasure than anything else. It wasn't until after she had divorced in the mid-1960s and moved to New York City that she thought seriously about developing one of the stories into a novel. She wrote in the evenings; during the day she edited textbooks for Random House Publishing Group. In 1970 her book The Bluest Eye was released to critical acclaim.

She followed that success with Sula in 1973. But it was her 1977 Song of Solomon that firmly established her as a major writer and garnered her a National Book Critics Circle Award for fiction. Each of her books won more praise and readers than the previous. Her success continued with Tar Baby (1981), Beloved (1987), Playing in the Dark (1992), and Paradise (1998). Morrison is a born storyteller. Her characters crackle with intensity and leap off the page. The stories affirm and portray a Black culture that is truly African-American, but her sensitive and personal observations of life succeed in crossing cultural boundaries.

Morrison's early success as a writer helped propel her career with Random House. She became a senior editor and stayed with the publishing house for 20 years. Her position allowed her to cultivate and encourage Black authors, bringing the African-American voice to millions of readers. In 2003, as a professor of humanities at Princeton University, Morrison continued to set the pace in the literary world by inspiring African Americans—and others—to look past the superficial and to reveal the greatest truth in their work and in their lives. She stated in a 1977 interview that "it seemed to [her] that Black people's grace is what they do with language."

a t the close of the 20th century, two women followed in the footsteps of the 20th century's first great African-American female philanthropist, Madam C. J. Walker—and they continue to do so. Like Madam Walker, Oprah Winfrey and Camille Cosby have used their vast talents and great wealth to support causes in which they believe.

Oprah Winfrey, known the world over simply as "Oprah," was born in the small Mississippi farm town of Kosciuski in 1954. Bright and inquisitive, Winfrey learned her letters before she was three and entered the third grade when she was six. While living with her mother in Milwaukee—Winfrey's parents, never married, had separated—Winfrey was repeatedly sexually abused by a cousin and other males who were close to the family. As a result, Winfrey lashed out in anger—she ran away, lied, and more. Her mother, unable to handle the increasingly difficult child, sent Winfrey to live with her father in Nashville. Winfrey was 14 years old.

Oprah Winfrey poses with Dorothy Height, longtime leader of the National Council of Negro Women, at a 2002 gala in honor of outstanding African-American women. An actress, businesswoman, and the most popular talk-show host on the planet, Winfrey certainly fits the category. She uses her show to celebrate the joys and strengths of ordinary women and vet their problems. She also tackles controversial or political subjects with a unique blend of forthrightness and tact. Her success and talent have made her one of the wealthiest people in the world, and she gives generously of both her time and money.

Her father channeled Winfrey's energy into education. Winfrey flourished under his loving guidance and strict discipline. In high school she discovered that she loved being in front of an audience. While still in high school, she began her broadcasting career in radio; she moved to television in college.

In 1976, after a few stints as a television newscaster, Winfrey was given the chance to co-host Baltimore WJZ-TV's morning show, *People Are Talking*. She had found her medium. Critics and viewers loved her straight talk and down-home attitude. Women—and not just Black women—were drawn to Winfrey. The show's ratings climbed steadily. In 1984, Chicago's WLS-TV hired Winfrey to host its morning show, *A.M. Chicago*. Within three years, the show was renamed *The Oprah Winfrey Show*, was syndicated in more than 190 cities, and had become the number one daytime talk show in the country, assuring her an undisputed place in history. She showed women how to look to themselves for strength and how to become truly happy.

Winfrey's success continued with the formation of her company, Harpo Productions, Inc. The company's productions—among them *The Wedding*, *Before Women Had Wings*, the 1998 screenplay adaptation of Toni Morrison's *Beloved* (in which she starred), and *O, The Oprah Magazine*—allow Winfrey to get the word out on issues that she cares about deeply: slavery, apartheid, child abuse, concerns of the African-American community, and more. Winfrey has become one of America's most important and influential leaders in business and in the arts and entertainment: She is a role model to people both in and outside the entertainment field.

Winfrey continues to reign as daytime's top talk-show host. But she does not just present issues; she offers solutions and inspires people to better themselves and others. She believes that "you get from the world what you give to the world." She uses her visibility to raise people's conciousness to help others in need. In 1997, she established the

Angel Network and challenged her viewers to send her their spare change. To date, donations have exceeded 12 million dollars. The Network has given scholarships to more than 150 students, supported the construction of more than 200 homes through Habitat for Humanity, and funded 34 schools in 10 countries. Winfrey's philanthropic efforts through the show have been well publicized, but she also personally donates time and money to things she cares about. She has contributed thousands of dollars to historically Black universities and charities; she organized a "Little Sisters" program in a Chicago housing project; and she sponsors inner-city youths at college preparatory schools.

In addition, Winfrey has long supported the work of the National Council of Negro Women (NCNW) in its efforts to improve the lives of African-American women and their families. In 2002, the NCNW threw a fundraiser and 90th birthday party for its president emerita and chair, Dr. Dorothy I. Height. Of the more than five million dollars raised that evening, Winfrey pledged more than one million. The money was used to "burn the mortgage" on the NCNW's building, which stands on the site of a former slave market on Pennsylvania Avenue in Washington, D.C. Winfrey's varied professions as a talk-show host, actress, media executive, and businesswoman have brought new meaning to the word "success." Her private and public lives serve as inspiration to hundreds of thousands of Black women, who see in her their own possibilities.

Winfrey counts among her friends Camille Cosby. Cosby was born Camille Olivia Hanks in 1945 in Washington, D.C. In 1964 she wed aspiring comedian Bill Cosby; she put

her educational dreams on hold to raise the couple's five children. As Bill Cosby grew more successful, Camille Cosby took over managing the family finances, and later became chief executive of Cosby Enterprises. In the late 1970s, Camille Cosby returned to college. "Education empowers you…. Once I got in, I just kept going." She went on to get a doctorate in education from the University of Massachusetts at Amherst. Her 1992 dissertation examined the impact of racial stereotypes in television shows on young people.

Cosby's belief in the important and empowering effects of education on African Americans led her to convince her husband to support education. Together, she and

When singer-songwriter Erykah Badu (opposite) burst onto the music scene in 1997, she drew comparisons to the legendary jazz singer Billie Holiday. In truth, Badu's musical style is all her own, born of jazz, hip-hop, rhythm and blues, and innate groove. She has a stunning sense of personal style and has made the headwrap—symbol of generations of hard-working Black women—her signature piece. On Badu, power is beautifully claimed, much like the cowry shells (left) once used to purchase African slaves, now seen in Afrocentric jewelry and clothing.

MARY MORAN IN SIERRA LEONE, WITH HER ANCESTRAL PEOPLE, IN 1997

MARY MORAN

Her mother sang this African song, which has been traced to its roots in Sierra Leone. She traveled there in 1997 to meet Baindu Jabati of the Mende people—who sang the same words, from a funeral refrain carried by a young slave to the Americas centuries ago. "They took everything she had but her dignity," said Mary Moran, "and they couldn't take the song."

Everyone come together, let us struggle;
    the grave is not yet finished;
    let his heart be perfectly at peace.
Everyone come together, let us struggle;
    the grave is not yet finished;
    let his heart be very much at peace.
Sudden death focuses everyone's attention
    like a firing gun.
Sudden death focuses everyone's attention,
    oh elder, oh head of the family.

Bill Cosby have made numerous contributions over the years to organizations that support African-American universities and all educational opportunities for Blacks. In 1988, the couple made history in the world of philanthropy, and in Black philanthropy in particular, when they donated 20 million dollars to Spelman College in Atlanta, Georgia. It was the single largest individual donation ever made to a historically Black university. The prestigious Black women's college used the funds to construct a much-needed academic center—which bears Camille Cosby's name—and to endow a program of fine arts and humanities.

Cosby used her studies and her contacts in the media world to work toward dispelling negative Black images. She produced the 1995 inspirational documentary No Dreams Deferred, which details how a small catering company changed the lives of five young Black men for the better. She used her dissertation work to author the book Television's Imageable Influences: The Self-Perceptions of Young African-Americans. In 1995, she and producer Judith Rutherford James co-produced the Broadway play Having Our Say, based on the best-selling autobiographical book of the same name. The play about the Delaney sisters, two African-American professional women who each lived to be more than a hundred years old, offers a message of hope and victory to Black women everywhere. The play received three Tony nominations. Cosby and James also co-produced the CBS television version of the story. The movie was seen by millions of viewers, who found the story life-affirming.

The overwhelming support and love for the Delaney sisters' story prompted Cosby to co-found, with veteran television journalist Renée Poussaint, the National Visionary Leadership Project in 2000. The project video archives the life stories, wisdom, and heritage of nationally recognized African-American elders so that their legacies and words can inspire leadership in future generations of America's Black youth. This project, like so much of Cosby's work, reflects her passion to make the world a better place—to encourage Black people to give back to the Black community.

When the Cosbys made their extraordinary gift to Spelman College, Johnnetta Betsch Cole headed the institution. She was the first African-American woman to helm the prestigious women's college. Born in 1936, Cole led a privileged life in Jacksonville, Florida. Her maternal great-grandfather, Abraham Lincoln Lewis, co-founded the Afro-American Life Insurance Company of Jacksonville in 1901. Johnnetta was encouraged to emulate as a role model the Cole family friend, Mary McLeod Bethune. Cole visited her home and school in Daytona Beach many times while growing up.

A precocious student, Cole left Jacksonville at the age of 15 to attend Fisk University in Nashville, Tennessee. She transferred to Oberlin College in Ohio the following year. A course on racial and cultural minorities sparked her interest in sociology and anthropology. After graduating in 1957, she pursued a doctorate in cultural anthropology at Northwestern University. She married Robert Cole, a graduate student in economics, in 1960. Then Johnnetta Cole taught part-time at Washington State University while she worked on her dissertation, "Traditional and Wage Earning Labor in Liberia." She was awarded her Ph.D. from Northwestern in 1967.

Cole's focus in the years to come remained cultural anthropology, but she broadened it to include African-American and women's studies. Her scholarly research on race, gender, and class contributed to her being offered a tenured professorship at the University of Massachusetts at Amherst in 1970. While there she developed the Afro-American Studies program and served as provost of undergraduate education for two years. In 1983 she was named director of the Latin American and Caribbean Studies Program at Hunter College in New York. In 1986 she published the seminal work *All American Women: Lines That Divide, Ties That Bind*. It forced people to recognize that women's rights in America were largely focused on White, middle-class women. It made the case that there were other women in America—such as unwed teenage mothers, elderly Black Medicare recipients, and welfare mothers—whose concerns needed to be addressed by government and society.

In 1987, Spelman College in Atlanta chose Cole to be its new president. Cole accepted the honor because it gave her the opportunity to help Black women excel. "No matter where I turned, I saw a reflection of myself," she said. "I saw black women, women in leadership, women professors, women intellectuals—words we rarely put together. And one of my tasks was to make us so at ease with being black women that we could reach out to the rest of the world." Cole's appointment gained national attention not only because she was the first African-American female president of the private Black women's college in its 107-year history, but also because the Cosbys announced their stunning 20-million-dollar gift to the college at her inauguration. She soon became known as the "Sister President." Over the course of her ten years at Spelman, Cole created new opportunities for her students, including a mentorship program with Atlanta's business community and a volunteer outreach program. She also ran a record-breaking fundraising campaign. Its success insured the college's commitment to graduating women with the strength, self-confidence, and academic credentials to become leaders in the Black community and society as a whole.

Marching under the slogan
"Repentance, Resurrection and
Restoration," participants in
the Million Woman March,
held in Philadelphia on
October 25, 1997, cheer while
listening to a speaker. Hoping
to foster solidarity among
women of African descent,
the march's organizers must
have been thrilled when 1.5
million African-American
women turned out to march.
The women cheered loudest
when U.S. Congresswoman
Maxine Waters proclaimed
"America, be placed on notice.
We know who we are. We
understand our collective
power. Following today, we
will act on that power."

U.S. National Security Advisor Condoleezza Rice confers with U.S. Secretary of State Colin Powell during a NATO conference in Prague on November 20, 2002. One of President Bush's closest advisors, Rice is gracious yet confident in who she is and what she believes. "I am a realist," she told the National Review. "Power matters. But there can be no absence of moral content in American foreign policy." Born in segregated Birmingham in 1954, Rice no doubt feels the same about American domestic policy.

After leaving Spelman in 1997, Cole eventually took on the challenge of presiding over another small Black school for women, Bennett College in North Carolina. She continues to research, write, and inspire through her leadership.

Johnnetta Cole is just one of a small but growing number of Black women heading a university. Ruth Simmons is another. Simmons was born in 1945 into a large sharecropping family in Grapeland, Texas. She lived on a cotton farm, an upbringing far removed from the "ivory tower" halls of academia. Convinced that education would be her way out of poverty, she attended Dillard University, in New Orleans. She graduated summa cum laude in 1967. While an undergraduate, she had spent one year at Wellesley College, in New England. She thrived there, finding the atmosphere more nourishing and encouraging for freethinking African-American women, and loving the all-women environment. She became convinced that her future lay in the North. She went to Harvard University for her doctorate degree in romance languages and literature. After she received it in 1973, she spent the next ten years teaching and holding the positions of assistant and associate dean at universities in Louisiana and California. But she never forgot her love of the Northeast.

When the position of acting director of the Afro-American Studies Program at Princeton University was offered to her in 1983, she jumped at the chance. She overhauled the program, hiring renowned experts such as Toni Morrison and Cornel West, and redirected its focus from political expression to intellectual query. The program became a role model for similar programs at universities around the country. The successful reorganization led to Simmons being appointed associate dean of Princeton's faculty. She became vice-provost at Princeton after she spent two years as provost at Spelman College. She authored a celebrated report on campus racism that has become known as the Simmons Report. Thanks to her recommendations, Princeton created an ombudsman's office to handle complaints and effected changes in its hiring practices and student recruitment. Many universities modeled changes in their operations on the recommendations in her report. Her reputation grew as an administrator with a unique perspective on the issues of race in higher education.

In 1995, Simmons was named president of prestigious Smith College in Northampton, Massachusetts. She was excited to work in an environment that catered to and encouraged women. She wanted to help women fully realize their potentials and never accept the status quo of a male-dominated society. She established an engineering program, the first of its kind at a women's college in the country, and launched *Meridiens*, a journal addressing the concerns of minority women. The students thrived under her leadership.

In 2000, Brown University wooed Simmons away from Smith to become its president. In accepting the position, she became the first Black woman president of an Ivy League school. Simmons earned her appointment and does not intend to curtail her beliefs—"I'm not going to be a symbolic president for Brown. I expect my hands will be in more things than people want."—in her quest to better higher education and make it available to all. She continues to lead with integrity and great vision for students of all colors.

The new millennium saw many Black women taking leadership roles on the world stage. Africana women were excelling in countries throughout Africa and the diaspora. In the United States, in 2001, Condoleezza Rice took the helm of the National Security Council (NSC), making her the first female and the first African-American National Security Advisor to the President of the United States.

She is a respected political scientist with an expertise in arms control and disarmament, specializing in the Soviet Union and Eastern Europe. Prior to her appointment, she had been on the faculty of Stanford University. In addition she had served as a special assistant to the director of the Joint Chiefs of Staff and later as a senior director at the NSC. However, when President George W. Bush named her his National Security Advisor, some people in the media were critical, pointing out Rice's inexperience in matters not related to the Soviet Union and the Cold War. Undeterred by the criticism, Rice has proven herself a savvy advisor and an indispensable member of President Bush's inner circle.

She was instrumental in crafting the President's War on Terrorism following the tragedies of September 11, 2001. The December 16, 2002, cover of *Newsweek* magazine featured a photograph of Rice with the following headline: "The Real Condi Rice: The Most Powerful Woman in Washington Is Black, Brainy and Bush's Secret Weapon." During the 2003 War on Iraq, Rice assisted the President in various ways behind the scenes. She speaks for the President and, while it is uncertain how much she influences his decisions, many Washington insiders believe she has "ultimate clout."

Occasionally Rice had the opportunity to interact with Sheila Sisulu, South Africa's ambassador to the U.S. Sisulu arrived in Washington, D.C., in 1999 and quickly gained the respect of the diplomatic community and the Black community. As ambassador, she graciously represented her country with intelligence and poise, and deftly handled relations between her country and the U.S. During her tenure, she was the spokeswoman for her country's difficult and sometimes controversial trials for reconciliation, as well as for the stand taken by her president, Thabo Mbeki, in the worldwide discussions regarding the AIDS virus and related issues.

Committed to the advancement of women, Sisulu eagerly accepted speaking engagements that allowed her to discuss the role of women around the world in politics and women's issues, including women's education. She broadened America's perceptions of African women, and of South African women in particular. In 2002 she gave a compelling talk at Georgetown University about the cultural norms within her country and how those norms affected a woman's willingness to take drugs to combat AIDS. At a White House summit of Black women in December 2000, "Africana Women at the Dawn of the New Millennium," she recounted the little-known story of how Black South African women played a major role in abolishing legalized apartheid.

By the time her term as ambassador had ended in 2003, she had made inroads into the African-American community by participating in Black women's events and Black college programs, and by attending Black social affairs. Sisulu is well respected for her candor and her intellect. She continues to fight for her people in the forefront of this new millennium. She is now the deputy executive director for the United Nations World Food Programme.

Sisulu is not the only woman from southern Africa working to improve the condition of people's lives. Graça Machel holds the distinction of having been First Lady of both Mozambique and South Africa, but she has done more than serve as a wife to

Artist Synthia Saint James displays her original artwork for a Kwanzaa stamp commissioned by the U.S. Postal Service that became available in 1997. Kwanzaa is a seven-day African-American holiday at the end of the year that celebrates seven principles: unity, collective work and responsibility, faith, cooperative economics, self-determination, purpose, and creativity. An accomplished and prolific artist, Saint James was a fitting choice for the Kwanzaa stamp, given that much of her art has explored African-American themes and subject matter.

presidents. Machel was born in 1945 in Portuguese East Africa (present-day Mozambique). In the early 1970s, while on scholarship to the University of Lisbon in Portugal, she joined the opposition group Front for the Liberation of Mozambique (FRELIMO).

In 1973, she returned to Africa and participated in preliminary measures to secure independence for her country. Because she was highly educated, the FRELIMO leaders assigned her to teach at one of the group's schools. She became a trusted and valued member of FRELIMO; she helped in the final negotiations for Mozambique's independence in 1974. In 1975 she married Samora Machel, one of the FRELIMO leaders whom she had met early in the war. When he became president of Mozambique that same year, he named her the minister of education—the only female cabinet member in the newly liberated Mozambique.

Cathy Freeman of Australia celebrates her Olympic gold medal victory in the women's 400 meter race at the 2000 Summer Games in Sydney. A world-class athlete, Freeman is also a proud, passionate, and pioneering spokeswoman and role model for her people, Australia's Aborigines.

Following pages: American rhythm and blues artist Alicia Keys performs with South African music legend Miriam Makeba (second from right) in Cape Town, South Africa, in November 2002. Makeba brought world attention to South African music and to her homeland's struggle against apartheid.

When Machel took charge, the total adult illiteracy rate was 90 percent. Within ten years, she had promoted universal elementary education and instituted sweeping changes to bring her country out of poverty. The number of students doubled and the illiteracy rates dropped to 45 percent for men and 78 percent for women. Following her husband's death in a plane crash in 1986, the deeply bereaved Machel carried on her commitment to Mozambique's children. The civil war of the past few years had destroyed nearly half of the country's schools and health care facilities. She worked to reestablish the infrastructure and to improve the lot of women and children—in the process raising the morale in Mozambique.

Machel resigned her ministerial post in 1989. In the next years she took posts on the international stage. In 1994, the United Nations commissioned Machel to study the impact of armed conflict on children. Her 1996 report exposed the harmful effects of war on children and "set the world agenda for child protection in situations of armed conflict." The work she did strengthened her resolve to help children.

> I have always believed it is our responsibility as adults to give children futures worth having. In the two years spent on this report, I have been shocked and angered to see how shamefully we have failed in this responsibility.... This process has strengthened my conviction that we must do anything and everything to protect children, to give them priority and a better future.

To this end, Machel established in Mozambique the Foundation for Community Development, a nonprofit organization that aims to eliminate poverty while protecting the most vulnerable in society—women and children. Machel's organization has improved the lives of countless Mozambicans and has served as a model for other groups and governments.

Machel continued to head the foundation even after she married longtime friend Nelson Mandela, the President of South Africa, in July 1998. Her tenure as First Lady of South Africa lasted only a year, since Mandela stepped down in 1999. Yet Machel's commitment to children has never wavered. In 2003, as the spokesperson for the Global Movement for Children, she continued her campaign for the young.

Machel, Winfrey, Angelou, and all Africana women today offer the new millennium great promise, as they play a vital role in setting the pace for the world to follow. In many ways, their story is just beginning. ♀

Ethiopia's queens
will reign again.

—Amy Ashwood Garvey

africana woman: her time line

"Ndebele Lady," by Sharon Reese

Uplifted by your victory
And heightened inner-seeing
Shape-shifting into mystery
You mastered the art of being
enlightened.

–From "The Art of Being" by Maia Thandeka Carroll
In honor of Lorilyn Simkins Daniels, who died in
March 2003; in honor of Hilda Taylor, former teacher
and NGS Alliance member, who perished on
September 11, 2001; and in honor of the ancestors,
who left us great knowledge and who guide us all.

chapter one: royalty

Queen Hatshepsut (ca 1500-1458 B.C.): Egyptian queen who crowned herself pharaoh, 1473-1458 B.C.

Queen Tiye (ca 1400-1340 B.C.): Egyptian queen from Nubia, believed to be ancestor of King Tutankhamun, married Amenhotep III.

Makeda, Queen of Sheba (tenth century B.C.): Wise queen of Ethiopia who bore Menilek I, son of Jerusalem's King Solomon.

The Candaces (ca 700s B.C.): Warrior women and queens of Kush in Africa, ruled circa the 25th dynasty, which was led by Egypt's Black Pharaohs.

Yennenga (ca A.D. 1100s): Mother of the Mossi people in present-day Ghana, married a prince from Mali.

Anna de Sousa Nzinga (1581-1663): Warrior queen of Ndongo (Angola).

Amina Kulibali (ca late 1600s): Daughter of King Wade Amedou of Kaharta, southeast Senegal, whose descendants founded the dynasty of Gabu, near Gambia.

Nandi (1770s-1827): South African mother of the Zulu warrior Shaka Zulu.

Queen Yaa Asantewa of Asante (ca 1850-1920): Led her people in battle against the British in 1900.

chapter two: from africa to the new world

Nanny, Queen of the Maroons (ca 1690-1750): Legendary revolutionary slave leader in Jamaica, led successful battles against the British in the First Maroon War, 1720-1739.

Coincoin (1742-1816): Prosperous landowner and slaveholder, born near New Orleans, although baptised Marie-Thérèse, born Coincoin, or "Second Daughter" in the Ewe language.

Queen Charlotte Sophia (1744-1818): Born in Germany, reigned beside her husband, King George III of England.

Phyllis Wheatley (ca 1753-1784): Prodigy poet, published a book, invited to read for George Washington.

Zeferina (ca late 1700s): Brazilian revolutionary, fought the Portuguese in 1826.

Nancy Prosser (ca late 1700s): Planned slave revolt, which was ultimately aborted, with her husband, Gabriel Prosser, near Richmond, Virginia, in 1800.

Sally Hemings (1773-1835): Half-sister to Martha Wayles Jefferson, wife of Thomas Jefferson, reportedly mother of at least one of Jefferson's children and perhaps five others.

Catherine "Katy" Ferguson (ca 1770-1854): Opened Katy Ferguson's School in Manhattan for Black and White street children and unwed mothers, ca 1793.

Mary Prince (ca late 1700s): Born in Bermuda, the first African-British slave who escaped bondage, published the first record of slavery.

Anastácia (ca 1800s): Slave and martyr, revered as a saint, especially by some Black women of Brazil.

Nancy Morejón (1944-): Author of poetry collections and acclaimed critical writings, born in Havana, Cuba.

chapter three: out of slavery

Tituba (ca late 1600s): Slave in Salem, Massachusetts, born in Barbados, considered cause of Salem Witch Trials, some scholars believe she was not Black but an American Indian.

Elizabeth Mumbet Freeman (ca 1742-1829): Slave who sued for her freedom and won it plus 30 shillings in an historic civil rights case in Massachusetts in the early 1780s.

Sojourner Truth (1797-1883): Abolitionist, women's rights activist.

Emily and Mary Edmonson (1800s): Slaves and sisters foiled in an escape attempt aboard the ship *Pearl*, later attended Oberlin College.

Mary Seacole (1805-1881): Jamaica-born nurse, set up boardinghouses and nursed wounded soldiers in war zones during Crimean War.

Ellen Craft (1826-1891): In a daring escape to freedom, posed as a sickly slave owner, traveling with her husband, who posed as her slave.

Harriet Tubman (ca 1831-1913): Inspirational conductor of the Underground Railroad.

Charlotte Forten Grimké (1837-1914): Born to wealthy Philadelphia abolitionists, taught in the Sea Islands.

Diana Fletcher (ca mid-1800s): Artist, a Black Indian of the Kiowa Nation, born to an escaped slave man and a Seminole woman, attended Hampton Institute.

Susie Baker King Taylor (1848-1912): Civil War nurse, only Black woman to publish memoirs of the war.

chapter four: making a place in the world

Clara Brown (1800-1885): Ran boardinghouses, made her fortune in Denver, Colorado, during the gold rush, financed wagon trains to bring Black people from the South to the West.

Mary Ellen Pleasant (ca 1810-1904): San Francisco entrepreneur and investor, abolitionist, and civil rights activist.

Elizabeth Keckley (1818-1907): Dressmaker, confidante of First Lady Mary Todd Lincoln in the Civil War White House.

Bridget "Biddy" Mason (1818-1891): Real estate magnate, first Black female property owner in Los Angeles, helped Black settlers in West.

Frances E. W. Harper (1825-1911): Abolitionist, writer, women's rights activist.

Mary Fields (1830-1913): Independent woman who was first Black female U.S. letter carrier, known as "Stagecoach Mary."

Charlotte Ray (1850-1911): First Black woman lawyer, practicing in Washington, D.C., from 1872 on.

Ida Bell Wells-Barnett (1862-1931): Journalist, antilynching activist.

Halle Tanner Dillon Johnson (1864-1901): First woman of any race to be licensed as a medical doctor, in Alabama in 1891.

Adelaide Smith Casely Hayford (1868-1960): Feminist, established first private secondary school for girls in Freetown, Sierra Leone, in the 1890s.

Carlotta Stewart-Lai (1881-1952): Raised in Brooklyn, taught in Hawaii for more than 40 years, principal of multiracial elementary school.

chapter five: taking society by storm

Gertrude Bustill Mosell (1855-1948): Quaker, abolitionist, women's rights activist.

Anna Julia Cooper (1858-1964): Educator, club woman, became president of Frelinghuysen University in 1930.

Mary Church Terrell (1863-1954): Educator and activist, led a boycott and court battle in 1953 to desegregate eateries in Washington, D.C.

Maggie Lena Walker (1867-1934): Motivational speaker, at the age of 37 founded the St. Luke Penny Savings Bank in Richmond, Virginia.

Madam C. J. Walker (1867-1919): Born Sarah Breedlove, philanthropist and entrepreneur of Black women's hair products.

Mary Jane McLeod Bethune (1875-1955): Activist, founder and president of Bethune College and of the National Council of Negro Women.

Nannie Helen Burroughs (1879-1961): Club woman, educator, women's rights activist.

Zora Neale Hurston (1891-1960): Writer, folklorist, playwright, author of autobiography highlighting the Harlem Renaissance.

Georgiana R. Simpson, Eva Dykes, Sadie Tanner Mossell Alexander (1921 graduates): The first Black women in the U.S. to earn a Ph.D.

Shirley Graham Du Bois (1896-1977): Writer, composer, conductor, playwright, director, wife of W. E. B. Du Bois, whose work she continued.

Eslanda Goode Robeson (1896-1965): With her husband, Paul Robeson, advocated self-determination for the colonized, particularly Africans.

Amy Euphemia Jacques Garvey (1896-1973): Journalist, second wife of Marcus Garvey, key developer of UNIA.

Amy Ashwood Garvey (1897-1969): With husband, Marcus Garvey, claims to have founded the Universal Negro Improvement Association (UNIA).

chapter six: speaking out

Augusta Savage (1892-1962): Sculptor during the Harlem Renaissance, work includes "La Citadelle Freedom."

Bessie Coleman (1896-1926): Aviator, educated and licensed in Europe but returned to U.S. and became daredevil stunt flyer.

Sadie Tanner Mosell Alexander (1898-1989): Second African-American woman to earn a Ph.D., first to earn it in economics, first African-American woman to practice law in Pennsylvania.

Dorothy Celeste Boulding Ferebee (1898-1980): Physician, director of health services, Howard University, head of various organizations including National Council of Negro Women.

Septima Poinsette Clark (1898-1987): Educator; Civil Rights activist, director of training camp for community activists.

Marian Anderson (1902-1993): World-renowned vocalist, performed on the steps of the Lincoln Memorial in 1939 for an audience of 75,000.

Ella Baker (1903-1986): Businesswoman, voting and Civil Rights activist.

Pauli Murray (1910-1985): Lawyer, professor, minister, feminist, poet.

Dorothy Height (1912-): Civil Rights activist, YWCA official, president emerita and chair of the National Council of Negro Women.

Rosa Parks (1913-): Civil Rights activist, spearheaded bus boycott in Montgomery, Alabama, 1950s, spurring changes in segregation law.

Dovey Roundtree (1914-): Joined the Women's Auxiliary Army Corps (WAAC) in 1942, one of first Black women in the U.S. military.

Fannie Lou Townsend Hamer (1917-1977): Activist, co-founder of Mississippi Freedom Democratic Party, aided 1965 Voting Rights Act.

Mattiwilda Dobbs (1925-): Opera singer, performing worldwide, including command performances for British and Swedish royalty.

Hazel Johnson Brown (1927-): First African-American female U.S. Army general, appointed in 1979.

Coretta Scott King (1927-): Civil Rights activist, founder of the Martin Luther King, Jr., Center for Nonviolent Social Change.

Ruby Blackburn (1933-1982): Voting and Civil Rights activist.

Azie Taylor Morton (1936-): U.S. Treasurer under President Carter.

Mary Frances Berry (1938-): Scholar, political activist, leader of the U.S. Civil Rights Commission.

Angela Davis (1944-): Activist, educator, freedom fighter, feminist.

chapter seven: Leaders on the world stage

Lois Mailou Jones (1905-1998): Artist, educator, winning awards for her contemporary paintings with African and Haitian themes.

Carolina Maria de Jesus (1913-): Best-selling Brazilian author.

Martha K. Cobb (1917-2002): Scholar of Afro-Hispanic literature, formative influence in crosscultural studies of Black literature.

Albertina Sisulu (1918-): South African freedom fighter, wife of the late Walter Sisulu, former leader of the African National Congress.

Shirley Anita Saint Hill Chisholm (1924-): First Black U.S. Congresswoman, Democrat from New York.

Mum Shirl Smith (1924-1998): Aided Aboriginal prisoners in Australia.

Mariama Ba (1929-1981): Women's rights activist, writer, from Senegal.

Rosemary Brown (1930-2003): Jamaican-born, first Black female member of the Canadian Legislature.

Yvonne Brathwaite Burke (1932-): U.S. Congresswoman, Democrat from California, elected in 1972.

Eleanor Holmes Norton (1937-): Lawyer, educator, Washington, D.C., delegate to U.S. House of Representatives.

Maxine Waters (1938-): U.S. Congresswoman, Democrat from California, former head of the Congressional Black Caucus.

Sharon Pratt Dixon Kelly (1944-): First female mayor, Washington, D.C.

Carol Moseley-Braun (1947-): Senator, ambassador to New Zealand, appointed by President Clinton, U.S. presidential candidate in 2003.

Alexis Herman (1947-): U.S. Secretary of Labor under President Clinton.

Maryam Babangida (1948-): Former first lady of Nigeria, founded women's aid groups, including the Better Life Program for the Rural Woman.

Sylvie Kinigi (1953-): Burundi's first woman prime minister, 1993-94.

Wilma Lewis (1956-): U.S. Attorney for the District of Columbia under President Clinton.

Anita Hill (1956-): Educator, testified in controversial Senate hearings to approve Clarence Thomas as Supreme Court Justice, now on faculty at Brandeis University.

chapter eight: setting the pace in the new millennium

Anita Johnson Mackey (1914-): Pioneer and longest-standing licensed clinical social worker in California; started Black cultural programs.

Mary Moran (1919-): Reunited with her ancestral people in Sierra Leone in the 1990s, recovered a song from her Sea Islands childhood.

Maya Angelou (1928-): Pulitzer Prize–winning writer, educator, actress.

Lady Gloria Hyacinth Blackman (1935-): Leader of women's organizations, wife of former ambassador to U.S. from Barbados.

Toni Morrison (1931-): Novelist and Pulitzer Prize–winning author.

Mariam Makeba (1932-): South African performer, social activist.

Mona Bailey (1932-) 17th Nat'l. President, Delta Sigma Theta Sorority.

Johnnetta Cole (1936-): President of Bennett College, former president of Spelman College.

Anne Clare Cools (1943-): Born in Barbados, member of Canadian Senate, focusing on family issues.

Judith Jamison (1943-): Dancer, choreographer, artistic director of Alvin Ailey Dance Theater.

Vashti Murphy McKenzie (1944-): First woman bishop in the African Methodist Episcopal church.

Alice Walker (1944-): Author of novels, poems, short stories, essays, and other works, including The Color Purple, winner of the Pulitzer Prize and the American Book Award.

Camille Cosby (1945-): Social activist, director, philanthropist, wife of Bill Cosby.

Shirley Franklin (1945-): First Black female mayor of Atlanta.

Ruth Simmons (1945-): Former president of Smith College, first Black president of Brown University.

Georgia Dunston (1945-): Geneticist, founding director of Howard University's Human Genome Center.

Graça Machel (1946-): Former first lady of two nations, Mozambique and then South Africa, wife of Nelson Mandela, children's advocate.

Nana Konadu Agyeman-Rawlings (1948-): Former first lady of Ghana, founder of 31st December Movement to address women's issues.

Constance Downing (1948-): First Black director of finance, Fairfax County Public Schools, Fairfax, Virginia.

Sheila Sisulu (1948-): Former South African Ambassador to the United States, 1999-2002, deputy executive director of the UN World Food Programme.

Synthia Saint James (1949-): Artist, illustrator, author, songwriter.

Alexa Canaday (1950-): One of the world's first Black female neurosurgeons.

Dolores Edwards (1951-): First Black female systems integration test engineer, working for Motorola.

Diane Abbott (1953-): First Black woman elected to British Parliament.

Adriane Dorrington (1954-): First indigenous African-Canadian woman from Nova Scotia to earn a doctorate in education, 1995.

Condoleezza Rice (1954-): National Security Advisor under President George W. Bush.

Oprah Winfrey (1954-): Television host, publisher, philanthropist, and businesswoman.

Charlotte Ramsey Gunaseharan (1955-): Village attorney, Spring Valley, New York.

Lark McCarthy (1955-): Television anchor, Fox-5 News, in Washington, D.C.

Angela, Princess of Liechtenstein (1956-): Former New York fashion designer, married Prince Maximilian in 2000.

Pamela Gordon (1956-): Premier of Bermuda, 1997-1998, youngest ever and first female elected to the post.

Mae Jemison (1956-): Chemical engineer, first Black female astronaut.

Gwendolyn Boyd: 22nd President, Delta Sigma Theta Sorority.

Linda M. White: Supreme Basileus, Alpha Kappa Alpha Sorority.

Helen J. Owens: Int'l. Grand Basileus, Sigma Gamma Rho Sorority.

Barbara C. Moore: Int'l Grand Basileus, Zeta Phi Beta Sorority.

Halle Berry (1968-): Academy Award–winning actress.

Queen Latifah (1970-): Rap artist, actress, appearing in numerous television shows and films, nominated for Academy Award, 2003.

Jada Pinkett Smith (1971-): Actress, acting in more than 20 films, established a production company, 100% Womon.

Erykah Badu (1971-): Award-winning rhythm and blues performer.

Cathy Freeman (1973-): Track star, indigenous Australian, Olympic gold medal winner.

Marion Jones (1975-): Sprinter, Olympic champion.

Venus and Serena Williams (1980- , 1981-): Sisters and international tennis champions, holding more than 25 and 19 titles respectively.

Alicia Keys (1981-): Grammy Award–winning singer.

Toshika Hudson, Renee Hypolite, Natosha Mitchell, Geneive Hardney, Lesjanusar Peterson, Adrienne Watson, Jamey McCloud (2002 graduates): First Black female cadet graduates from The Citadel.

endnotes Credits for noted quotes.

Introduction:

7 from "And Still I Rise": Maya Angelou, courtesy Random House.

Chapter 1:

14 "In ancient times": Harold Courlander, from *The Piece of Fire*, Harcourt; 25 "I have done this with a loving heart": Miriam Lichtheim, *Ancient Egyptian Literature*, 27; 26 "It is you who knows better": William L. Moran, *The Amarna Letters*, 84; 31 "If I follow you": Simone Schwarz-Bart, *In Praise of Black Women 1: Ancient African Queens*, 140; 38 "Oh you": Andrzewski & Lewis. *Somali Poetry: An Introduction*.

Chapter 2:

47 "Involuntarily I strolled": Anna Maria Falconbridge, *Narrative of Two Voyages to the River Sierra Leone 1791-1793*, 21; 52 "All those who have good legs": Simone Schwarz-Bart, *In Praise of Black Women 2: Heroines of the Slavery Era*, 26; 59 "Black Woman": Nancy Morejon, from *Where the Island Sleeps Like A Wing*, Black Scholar Press, 1984, trans. Karen Weaver, 86-89; 61 "Nanny of the Maroons": Tom Clynes, "Blue Mountain Mystery," *NG Adventure*, 122; 61 "I, as the eldest, stood first": Mary Prince, *The History of Mary Prince, a West Indian Slave*, 52; 65 "No sooner had I heard of war": Mary Seacole, *Wonderful Adventures of Mary Seacole in Many Lands*, 73.

Chapter 3:

71 "Lineage": Margaret Walker Alexander, from *This is My Century*, University of Georgia Press; 74 "The devil came to me": Paul Boyer, *Salem Witchcraft Papers...of 1692*, 747; 81 "reluctantly driven to the sad" and "I think it is almost": William and Ellen Craft, *Running a Thousand Miles For Freedom*, 29-30; 92 "I was very happy": Susie Taylor, *A Black Woman's Civil War Memoirs*, 21; 94 "How exciting": from Charlotte Forten Grimké diaries, Grimké Collection., ctsy Moorland-Spingarn Research Center, Howard University.

Chapter 4:

99 from "Ruth": Pauli Murray, from *Dark Testament*, Silvermine; 105 "Through weary, wasting": Frances Harper, "Woman's Political Future," *The World's Congress of Representative Women*, 433-37; 107 "I rented apartments" and "If the white people": Elizabeth Keckley, *Behind the Scenes...*, 65, 107; 117 "the kind of old friend": "Clara Brown," AFRO-American Almanac website (www.toptags.com/aama/ index); 122 "Time was when the country": Ida B. Wells-Barnett, letter to Anti-Lynching Bureau, Jan. 1, 1902, Daniel Murray Pamphlet Coll., Library of Congress; 124 from "To Black Women": Gwendolyn Brooks, Reprinted By Consent of Brooks Permissions.

Chapter 5:

132 "If our women want": Maggie Lena Walker, "Traps for Women," speech at Bethel A.M.E. Church, Richmond, VA, March 15, 1925, Maggie Lena Walker Natl. His. Site, NPS; 136 "I have been trying": A'Lelia Bundles, *On Her Own Ground*, 135; 137 "I had devoured what" and 140 "Let our girls feel": Anna J. Cooper, *A Voice from the South*, 76-79; 146 "I could not be happy" and "All during my college": Mary Church Terrell, *A Colored Woman in a White World*, 59-60; 153 "This in itself": Mary McLeod Bethune, "A Philosophy of Education for Negro Girls," *Building a Better World*, 85;

154 "The principle of justice": Mary McLeod Bethune, "Closed Doors," *Building a Better World*, 211-12.

Chapter 6:

162 "In principle the idea": Marian Anderson, *My Lord, What a Morning*, 189; 164 "People always say": Rosa Parks, *My Story*; 166 "In our family": "A Voice for the Disadvantaged," *Washington Post*, May 5, 1978; 162 "the poor, the old": "A Voice for the Disadvantaged," *Washington Post*, May 5, 1978; 167 "the presence of the segregated": letter to Pres. Harry S. Truman, July 19, 1951, Desegregation of the Armed Forces Document Collection, Harry S. Truman Presidential Library; 169 "From the time the first black people": Coretta Scott King, Epilogue from *And Still We Rise*, by Barbara Reynolds, ctsy Martin Luther King Ctr.; 174 "I done paid my dime": "The Little Girl Would Not Move," Microsoft Encarta Africana; 175 "When I made that decision": Douglas Brinkley, *Rosa Parks*, 107; 178 "the work the women did": Tonya Bolden, *The Book of African-American Women*, 284; 187 "If Rosa Parks": from *I Dream A World: Portraits...*, Photographs and Interviews by Brian Lanker © 1999, Stewart, Tabori, and Chang. Used with permission. All rights reserved.

Chapter 7:

195 "unite and form a solid": Coretta Scott King, speech, Washington, D.C., June 19, 1968, ctsy Martin Luther King Ctr.; 195 "high rates of child poverty": Founder's Message, at www.thekingcenter.org, ctsy. Martin Luther King Ctr.; 196 "I guess these words": Coretta Scott King, St. Paul Academy commencement speech, June 10, 2001, ctsy Martin Luther King Ctr.; 197 "Prejudice against blacks": Shirley Chisholm, to the House of Representatives, May 21, 1969; 199 "My grandfather was a Cherokee": Yvonne Brathwaite Burke, Carter interview, 2003; 200 "I am not the candidate": "Against Great Odds...", *Chicago Tribune*, Feb. 19, 2003; 205 "Whether the issue is": "U.S. Rep. Maxine Waters," *Freedom Magazine*, 29: 1, 28; 211 "There are those who": Carol Moseley-Braun, to U.S. Senate, 1993; 213 "I have raised my voice": Carol Moseley-Braun, speech prepared for DNC Winter Meeting 2003, at www.carolforpresident.com; 213 "I will never forget": Alexis Herman, to U.S. Conference of Mayors, June 24, 1997, at gos.sbc. edu; 214 "Because of the 22.5 million": Alexis Herman, remarks to Department of Labor, January 11, 2001, at www.dol.gov; 216 "I have learned": Darlene Clark Hine, from *Black Women in America*.

Chapter 8:

218 "Be mindful": Mona Humphries Bailey, *Delta Sigma Theta Journal*; 225 "We need to see": "Maya Angelou," Biography Resource Center, from Claudia Tate's *Black Women Writers at Work*; 228 "it seemed to her": "Morrison, Toni," *Africana Encyclopedia*, 1343; 230 "you get from the world": Oprah Winfrey, Angel Network pages, Oprah.com; 231 "Education empowers you": "Camille Cosby," Biography Resource Center, as quoted in an *American Visions* article; 233 "Everyone come together": Mary Moran interviews: NGM 1997, NG Books 2003; 235 "No matter where": "Johnnetta Cole. Challenging the Status Quo," *Emory Magazine*, 1998; 239 "I'm not going to be symbolic": "Making History," *Brown Alumni Mag.* Jan./Feb. 2001; 242 "I have always believed": Graça Machel, UNICEF website, "Impact of Armed Conflict on Children" (www.unicef.org/graca/).

authors

Historian **Dr. Cynthia Jacobs Carter** is director of development at Howard University and an adjunct professor at Georgetown University and The George Washington University (GWU), where she is an instructor in women's studies. From GWU she holds a doctorate in education and a master's degree in international education. She holds a B.S. in business education from Virginia State University. Dr. Carter served as an alliance coordinator for the District of Columbia Geographic Alliance from 1994 to 1997 and as an educational consultant for the National Geographic Society from 1992 to 1994. She has designed and taught several courses on such topics as "Black Women in the African Diaspora" and "The Gullah Culture." In 1999 she founded the Africana Women's Nexxus Institute in Washington, D.C., and has developed and coordinated several exhibitions through the institute, including "Africana Woman at the Dawn of the New Millennium," sponsored by the White House Millennium Council and GWU. Dr. Carter is on the board of directors of the Delta Sigma Theta Sorority Research and Education Foundation (DREF) and the National MultiCultural Institute. From Virginia's Eastern Shore, Dr. Carter now lives in Kingstowne, Virginia, with her husband, Karl W. Carter, Jr.

In her new book, *Open Wide The Freedom Gates: A Memoir*, **Dr. Dorothy Height** chronicles her remarkable life story as a civil rights and human rights activist, during which time she worked with such leaders as Mary McLeod Bethune, Martin Luther King, Jr., W. E. B. Du Bois, Marcus Garvey, Adam Clayton Powell, Sr., Eleanor Roosevelt, A. Phillip Randolph, Roy Wilkins, and many others. Born in Richmond, Virginia, Dr. Height earned her undergraduate and graduate degrees from New York University. She proceeded to work in leadership roles with the Young Women's Christian Association (YWCA), the Center for Racial Justice, Delta Sigma Theta Sorority, Inc., and the National Council of Negro Women (NCNW). Dr. Height holds numerous honorary degrees and has been awarded the Presidential Medal of Freedom, the Franklin Delano Roosevelt Freedom Medal, and the Citizens Medal Award. She has advised United States Presidents from Dwight D. Eisenhower to Bill Clinton. She continues to make a difference in the lives of millions of people, and in particular, she dedicates herself to improving the lives of ordinary families. After more than 40 years, she continues to lead the National Council of Negro Women as Chair and President Emerita. She lives in Washington, D.C.

acknowledgments

My doctoral dissertation, "Higher Education and the Talented Tenth," nearly ten years ago, was the starting point for this book—a journey to celebrate and elucidate the story of Africana Women. From it I developed an exhibition, with the help of Francine Henderson and Erica Aungst of The George Washington University (GWU) and Betty Kleckley Stratford of the National Council of Negro Women. "Africana Women at the Dawn of the New Millennium," cosponsored by the White House Millennium Council and the Gelman Library at GWU, profiled nearly 200 Black women and their contributions and included related programs, lectures, and a White House Summit.

In summer 2001, Barbara Brownell Grogan, Executive Editor with the National Geographic Book Division, upon my invitation, viewed the work at the Sumner School and Museum. That visit began an important leg in the journey: the making of this book, with its contribution by many great women.

I have profound appreciation for one such woman, Dr. Dorothy Height, who has lent her time, her wisdom, and the benefits of her experience to whatever project I have asked her to participate in. She graciously agreed to write the Introduction to this book, even while completing her own manuscript. Thanks to Dr. Height and to all the women who assisted her.

Thanks to my family for being so understanding: Connie, Eugene, Gene, and Victor Downing; Karl H., Janna, Clayton, and Nathaniel Carter, and their spouses. Thanks to my grandchildren, Muhammad and Zoë Byrd.

I am fortunate to have wonderful colleagues at Howard University, who supported me as I wrote this book. Thank you one and all, especially Virgil Ecton, Love Collins, Dr. Thomas Battle, Jo Ellen El Bashir, and Donna Wells. Donna's insight and contributions to this book have been immeasurable.

My eternal gratitude goes to many talented, tenacious individuals at National Geographic, who were steadfast in the book's evolving process. I offer deep appreciation to Executive Editor and wordsmith extraordinaire, Barbara Brownell Grogan. I sincerely thank her for sharing my vision and for holding this work to the highest standards, so that Africana Woman would shine. Heartfelt thanks goes to these amazing people: Susan Blair, Jane Sunderland, Ruth Chamblee, Cinda Rose, Susan Hitchcock, Barbara Fallon, and Alison Reeves.

Very special thanks to the book's consultant, Marilyn Mobley McKenzie, of George Mason University, and Charles L. Blockson. Much appreciation goes to my Women's Studies colleagues, including Suzanna Walters of Georgetown University (GU), Diane Bell of GWU. Thanks also to Rosangela Maria Vieira of GU. Sincere gratitude goes to Dolores, Adriane, Helena, and Jolene for their support throughout. And I thank research facilities at Moorland-Spingarn Research Center, The National Museum of African Art at the Smithsonian Institution, National Geographic, The Charles L. Blockson Collection at Temple University, Georgetown University, The George Washington University, Auburn Avenue Research Library, and The Getty Museum.

Finally, thanks to my SGI-USA family for their encouragement, including Greg Martin, Pamela Leech, and Maia Carroll. Nam-myoho-renge-kyo.

—CYNTHIA JACOBS CARTER

additional sources

Janus Adams, Sister Days: 365 Inspired Moments in African American Women's History, John Wiley and Sons, Inc., 2000. • Kwame Anthony Appiah and Henry Louis Gates, Jr., Africana: The Encyclopedia of the African and African American Experience, Basic Civitas Books, 1999. • Tritobia Hayes Benjamin, The Life and Art of Lois Malou Jones, Pomegranate Artbooks, 1994. • Charles L. Blockson, Hippocrene Guide to the Underground Railroad, Hippocrene Books, Inc., 1994. • Tonya Bolden, And Not Afraid To Dare: The Stories of Ten African-American Women, Scholastic Press, 1998. • Tonya Bolden, The Book of African-American Women: 150 Crusaders, Creators, and Uplifters, Adams Media Corporation, 1997. • Margaret Busby, Daughters of Africa: An International Anthology of Words and Writings by Women of African Descent From the Ancient Egyptian to the Present, Ballantine Books, 1992. • Cynthia Jacobs Carter, Higher Education and the Talented Tenth at the New Millennium, Ed. D. Dissertation, The George Washington University, 1998. • David Coulson and Alec Campbell, African Rock Art: Painting and Engravings on Stone, Harry N. Abrams, Inc., 2001. • Adelaide M. Cromwell, An African Victorian Feminist: The Life and Times of Adelaide Smith Casely Hayford 1868-1960, Howard University Press, 1992. • Nancy C. Curtis, Ph.D., Black Heritage Sites: The South, The New Press, 1996. • Basil Davidson, African Civilization Revisited: From Antiquity to Modern Times, African World Press, Inc., 2001. • Miriam Decosta-Willis, The Memphis Diary of Ida B. Wells: An Intimate Portrait of the Activist as a Young Woman, Beacon Press, 1995. • Christiane Desroches-Noblecourt, Tutankhamen: Life and Death of a Pharaoh, Penguin Books, 1989. • Discovery Channel, The Real Eve, DVD, 2002. • Howard Dodson, Jubilee: The Emergence of African-American Culture, National Geographic, 2002. • W. E. B. Du Bois, The Education of Black People: Ten Critiques, 1906-1960, Monthly Review Press, 1973. • John Hope Franklin, Alfred A. Moss, Jr., From Slavery to Freedom: A History of African Americans, Alfred Knopf, Inc., 1994. • Paula Giddings, When and Where I Enter: The Impact of Black Women on Race and Sex in America, William Morrow and Company, 1984. • Karla Gottlieb, A History of Queen Nanny: Leader of the Windward Jamaican Maroons, Africa World Press, 2000. • Beverly Guy-Sheftall, Words of Fire: An Anthology of African-American Feminist Thought, The New Press, 1995. • Zahi Hawass, Silent Images: Women In Pharaonic Egypt, Henry N. Abrams, Inc., 2000. • Dorothy Height, Open Wide The Freedom Gates: A Memoir, Public Affairs, 2003. • Evelyn Brooks Higginbotham, Righteous Discontent: The Women's Movement in the Black Baptist Church, 1880-1920, Harvard University Press, 1993. • Patricia M. Hinds, 40 of the Most Inspiring African-Americans, Essence Books and Time Inc., 2002. • Darlene Clarke Hine, Elsa Barkley Brown, Rosalyn Terborg-Penn, Black Women in America: An Historical Encyclopedia, Indiana University Press, 1994. • bell hooks, Ain't I a Woman: Black Women and Feminism, South End Press, 1981. • bell hooks and Cornel West, Breaking Bread: Insurgent Black Intellectual Life, South End Press, 1991. • Nathan Irvin Huggins, Voices from the Harlem Renaissance, Oxford University Press, 1995. • Joy James, Transcending the Talented Tenth: Black Leadership and American Intellectuals, Routledge, 1997.

• Allison J. Keyes, Gloria Blakely, Charles R. Branham (consultant), Great African Americans, Publications International, Lt., 2002. • Brian Lanker, I Dream A World: Portraits of Black Women Who Changed America, Stewart, Tabori & Chang, 1989. • David Levering Lewis, W. E. B. Du Bois: A Reader, Henry Holt and Company, 1995. • Annette Madden, In Her Footsteps: 101 Remarkable Black Women from the Queen of Sheba to Queen Latifah, Conari Press, 2000. • Kenny Mann, Kingdoms of the Past: Kongo Ndongo, West Central Africa, Dillon Press, 1996. • The Mariners' Museum, Captive Passage: The Transatlantic Slave Trade and the Making of the Americas, Smithsonian Institution Press, 2002. • Audrey Thomas McCluskey and Elaine M. Smith, Mary McLeod Bethune: Building a Better World, Indiana University Press, 1999. • Microsoft Encarta, Africana 2000, 1993-1999. • Lynn Olson, Freedom's Daughters: The Unsung Heroines of the Civil Rights Movement from 1830 to 1970, Scribner, 2001. • G.M. Pomeranz, Where Peachtree Meets Sweet Auburn: The Saga of Two Families and the Making of Atlanta, Lisa Drew/Scribner, 1996. • Barbara Reynolds, And Still We Rise: Interviews with 50 Black Role Models, USA Today Books, Gannett News Media Services, Inc., 1988. • Helen C. Rountree, Pocahontas's People: the Powhatan Indians of Virginia Through Four Centuries, University of Oklahoma Press, 1990. • Simone Schwarz-Bart, André Schwarz-Bart, In Praise of Black Women 1: Ancient African Queens, University of Wisconsin Press, Modus Vivendi Publications, 2001. • Simone Schwarz-Bart, André Schwarz-Bart, In Praise of Black Women 2: Heroines of the Slavery Era, University of Wisconsin Press, Modus Vivendi Publications, 2002. • Ronald Segal, The Black Diaspora: Five Centuries of the Black Experience Outside Africa, The Noonday Press, 1995. • Saundra Sharp, Black Women for Beginners, Writers and Readers, 1993. • Jessie Carney Smith, Powerful Black Women, Visible Ink Press, 1996. • Joyce Tyldesley, Daughters of Isis: Women of Ancient Egypt, Penguin Books, 1995. • Ivan Van Sertima, They Came Before Columbus: The African Presence in Ancient America, Random House, 1976.

INDEX

Boldface indicates illustrations

Abaete, Lord 52, 56
Abolitionists 82, 85, **86**, 87, 88, 91, 92–94, 94, 101, 104, 109, 110, 111, 137, 140; *see also* Anti-slavery movement
Academy of Negro Youth, Baltimore, Md. 101
Adams, Abigail 80
Adams, John 80
Affirmative action 205, 214
Africa: birthplace of humanity 19; slave trade 43, **44–45**, 45, 47; *see also places by name*
Afro-American studies 235, 238–239
Ahmose-Nefertere, Queen 17, 20
Akhenaten (Amenhotep IV), Pharaoh (Egypt) 26–27
Alabama: bus boycotts 174–176; civil rights demonstrations 161, **172–173**, 173; segregation 174–176; slaves 108
Alexander, Margaret Walker: quoted 71
Alexander, Sadie Tanner Mossell 144, 170–171, 174
Algeria: cave painting **21**
Alpha Kappa Alpha 130, 166
Amazons **32–33**, 33
A.M.E. Church Review 170
Amenhotep III, Pharaoh (Egypt) 25–26
Amenhotep IV (Akhenaten), Pharaoh (Egypt) 26–27
American Civil Liberties Union (ACLU) 174
American Equal Rights Association 104
American Women Suffrage Association 105
Amistad (slave ship) 50
Anastácia (slave) 52, 56
Anderson, Marian 161–162, **163**, 164, 165, 166
Angelou, Maya 7, 221, **224**, 224–225, 252; quoted 7
Angola: royalty 34–35; slave trade 47
Anthony, Susan B. 104
Antislavery movement 82, 90, 101, 104; circular **72**, 73; societies 64, 91, 93, 104
Apartheid 141, 176, 196, 205, 230, 240
Asante **16**, 17, 36, **37**, 47, 56–57, 60
Asantewa, Yaa, Queen 36, **37**
Asia: slavery 45
Astronauts **222–223**, 223
Atlanta, Ga. 165, 166, 194, 197

Baartman, Saarti 66, **67**
Badu, Erykah **230**, 231
Bahia (Salvador), Brazil 52, 56
Bailey, Mona: quoted 218
Bance Island, Sierra Leone: slave trading fort 47, 50
Barbados 73; hotel tavern **60**, 61

Barnett, Ferdinand L. 122
Barton, Clara 92
"Beautiful Ladies" (rock carving) 36, **38–39**
Beck, Selma **148**, 149
Beecher, Henry Ward 91, 93
Bell, Dorothy 174, **175**
Bennett, Gwendolyn: quoted 41
Benin 52; slave trade 43
Bermuda: slaves 61, 64
Berry, Halle **220**, 221
Berry, Mary Frances: quoted 187
Bethune, Mary McLeod 136, 140, **140**, 149, 152–154, **155**, 166, 182, 184, 234; quoted 68, 157
Bilqis *see* Makeda, Queen of Sheba
Birmingham, Ala.: civil rights demonstrations **172–173**, 173; segregation 174–176
Black Eve (painting) **14–15**, 17
Black Indians **90**, 91, 111, **198**, 199
Black Madonna and Child (painting) **46**, 47
Black Power movement 181
"Black Woman" (Morejón) 59
Black Women's Club Movement 130, 133, 139, 146–147, 149, 153–154, 184
Brazil: slaves 51, 52, 55, 56, 62, **62–63**, 66, **68–69**
Breedlove, Sarah *see* Walker, Madam C. J.
Bridges, Ruby 166, **167**
Bridgetown, Barbados: hotel tavern **60**, 61
British: military 64, 65, 66; slaves 47, 49, 51, 56–57, 61, 64, 73
British Hotel, Balaclava, Turkey 66
Brooke, Edward W. 210
Brooks, Gwendolyn: quoted 124
Brown, Clara 116–117
Brown, Eliza Jane 117
Brown, George 116
Brown, John 110, 111
Brown v. Board of Education 176, 177
Bullock, Annie Mae *see* Turner, Tina
Burke, Yvonne Brathwaite 196, **198**, 199, 200, 204
Buses **186–187**; boycotts 164, 174–176, 184, 194
Bush, George H. W. (U.S. Pres.) 207
Bush, George W. (U.S. Pres.) 213, 239–240

California 110, 111, 112, 200, 204–206
Canady, Alexa **212**, 213
Candomblé **54–55**, 55, 56
Cape Coast Castle, Ghana: slave trading fort 47, 49
Carib-Indians 74
Caribbean 65; slavery 43, 45, 51, 73; woman with basket **42**
Carnival (festival) 66, **68–69**
Carter, Jimmy (U.S. Pres.) 164, 174

Cary, Mary Ann Shadd 109
Castles (slave trading forts) 47, **48–49**, 49, 50
Catholicism 34, 52, 55, 56, 76
Center for Racial Justice 184
Chad: rock carving 36, **38–39**
Chapman, Maria Weston 93
Chisholm, Shirley **194**, 195, 196–197, 200
Citizens Medal Award 184
Citizenship schools 177–178
Civil rights 111, 121–122, 130, 141, 146, 149
Civil Rights Movement 122, 154, 164–186, 191, 193–196, 213; demonstrations **158–160**, 161, 194
Civil War, U.S. 91–94, 136
Clark, Nerie 177
Clark, Septima Poinsette 176–178
Clinton, Bill (U.S. Pres.) 176, 184, 200, 213, 214, 220, **224**
Clothing 181; ceremonial **54–55**, 55; royalty 20; slaves 52, **53**, **62–63**; Sunday dress 11; traditional **4**, 5, **10**, 11, **16**, 17
Clubs *See* Black Women's Club Movement; Mother Clubs; Sororities
Code Noir 76, 77
Coincoin 76–77
Cole, Johnnetta Betsch **196**, 197, 234–235, 238
Coleman, Bessie 144, **145**
Colorado 116–117, 135
Colored Female Religious and Moral Society of Salem, Salem, Mass. 130
Colored Girls School, Washington, D.C. 91
Colored Women's League 146
Columbia Univ., New York, N.Y. 144, 164, 196
Colvin, Claudette 174–175
Congressional Black Caucus 204, 205
Congresswomen **188–190**, 191, **194**, 195, 196–197, **198**, 199–200, 204–206, 210–212
Contraband Relief Association 107
Coolidge, Ellen Randolph 80–81
Cooper, Anna Julia Hayward 137, **141**
Cosby, Bill 234
Cosby, Camille 228, 231, 234, 235
Cotton pickers **70–71**, 73, **102–103**, 103, 135
Council of Colored Women 133
Craft, Ellen 81–83
Craft, William 81–83
"Creole medical arts" 64
Crimean War 64, 65–66
Crummell, Alexander 137, 140
Cunningham, David 205

Dahomey, Kingdom of, West Africa: slave trade 43; women warriors **32–33**
Daughters of the American Revolution (DAR) 162

Davis, Varina Howell 107
Daytona Educational and Industrial Institute for Negro Girls 136, 140, **140**, 152–153, 234
de Soto, Marie de Nieges 76
de Sousa, Correia 34
de St. Denis, Louis Juchereau 76
Deities: female **29**, 52, 55, **55**, 56
Delaney sisters 234
Delta Sigma Theta (sorority) 130, 154, **156–157**, 171, 184
Desegregation 161; schools 149
Dillard Univ., New Orleans, La. 238; sororities 154, **156–157**
Dingiswayo 36
Dletsheni people 36
Dobbs, Mattiwilda 164–165
Douglass, Frederick 91, 141, 146
Draper, Elizabeth 132
Drayton, Dan 88
Dred Scott case (1857) 111
Du Bois, W. E. B. 122, 129–130, 140, 141, 144, 149
Dutch: slaves 47, 52, 73
Dykes, Eva B. 144

Edmonson, Amelia 83, 88, 91
Edmonson, Emily 88, 91
Edmonson, Mary 88, 91
Edmonson, Paul 83, 88, 91
Education 136–137, 140–141, 144–147, 149, 152–154, 166, 167; industrial 130, 133, 144; as means to betterment 91, 121, 129, 132, 146, 221; Talented Tenth 129–130, 144
Egypt, ancient 28; map 25; queens 17, 20–21, **22**, 23, 25–27, **27**, 28, **29**
Elom, Olufemi 11, **12–13**
England: slaves 64
Equal Rights Amendment 197, 200
Ethiopia: royalty 27–28; women **6–7**, 8
Falconbridge, Alexander 47, 50
Falconbridge, Anna Marie 47
Federal Council on Negro Affairs 154
Federation of Afro-American Women 146
Female Anti-Slavery Society of Salem 93
Ferebee, Dorothy Celeste Boulding 166, 170
Fields, "Stagecoach Mary" 112, **113**, 117, 120
15th Amendment 104, 129

Fillmore, Millard (U.S. Pres.) 82
First Maroon War (1720-39) 56
First South Carolina Volunteers 92–94, 94, **95**
Fisk University, Nashville, Tenn. 136, 235; Jubilee Singers **120**, 121
Fletcher, Diana **90**, 91
Florida: cotton pickers **102–103**; slaves 91

Forten, James, Sr. 92
Forten, Mary 93
Forten, Robert Bridges 93
14th Amendment 101, 129
Free Blacks 64–66, 82, 88, 92, 93, 107
Free states 109, 111
Freedmen's Bureau 91, 136
Freeman, Cathy 242, **243**
Freeman, Elizabeth Mumbet 77, **77**
French: slave trade 47, 51, 73
Fugitive Slave Act (1850) 82, 91
Fulani 21

Gabu, King of 31
Gambia 31
Garland family 105, 107
Garrison, William Lloyd 109
Garvey, Amy Ashwood: quoted 245
Georgia 149, 152, 166, 194; civil rights
    demonstrations **160**, 161; segregation
    165; slaves 81, 91–92
Ghana: royalty 28–29, 31; slave trade 43
Girl Scouts of the USA **148**, 149, 167
Gold rush 110, 116
Good, Sarah 74
Gorée Island, Senegal **10**, 51; slave
    trading fort 47, **48–49**, 49, 50
Goria 31
Grant, Mary Jane see Seacole, Mary
Great Depression 153, 154
"Great Migration" 143; see also
    Migrations: northward
Grimké, Charlotte Forten 92–94, 141
Griots (storytellers) 30, 34
Gsangomar 31
Gullah 92, 94

Haines Institute, Augusta, Ga. 149, 152
Hairstyles **16**, 17, **21**, 21, **62–63**, 134–136,
    180–181, 181; royalty 20, **22**
Hamble Town, Bermuda: slave market
    61, 64
Hamer, Fannie Lou Townsend 179, **179**,
    182; quoted 158
Hannah, Grace 115, **115**
Hannah, Truth **114**, 115
Harlem Renaissance 151
Harper, Frances Ellen Watkins 101, 104,
    104, 105, 141; quoted 97
Harrison, Benjamin (U.S. Pres.) 146
Hatshepsut, Queen (Egypt) 17, 20–21,
    22, 28
Hawaii 122
Health care 166, 170, 204, 210, 242
Height, Dorothy I. **9**, 154, 182, 184, 228,
    229, 231
Helms, Jesse 211, 213
Hemings, Elizabeth "Betty" 77
Hemings, Eston 81
Hemings, Madison 80, 81
Hemings, Sally 77, 80–81; bell **80**, 81
Henderson, Annie 220, 224

Herman, Alexis Margaret 213–214
Hill, Anita Faye 200, **201**, 206–207, 210
Hine, Darlene Clark: quoted 216
Holiday, Billie 231
Housewives' League of Detroit **152**, 153
Housing 132, 167, 200, 204, 210
Howard Univ., Washington, D.C. 91,
    122, **123–124**, 165, 166, 225, 228
Hunt, Ida Gibbs 137, 140
Hurston, Zora Neale **150–151**, 151;
    quoted 188

Ickes, Harold 162
Illinois 210–211, 213
Indians see Black Indians
Integration 130, 154, 174, 184
International Council of Women 149

Jabati, Baindu 233
Jackson, Jesse 195
Jackson, Maynard H. 166
Jamaica 200; currency 56, **57**; slaves
    56–57, 60, 61, 73; women 64–66
Jamestown, Va.: slaves 73
Jamison, Judith 214, **215**
Jefferson, Isaac 80
Jefferson, Lucy Elizabeth 80
Jefferson, Martha 80
Jefferson, Martha Wayles 77, 80; bell **80**, 81
Jefferson, Thomas (U.S. Pres.) 77, 80–81
Jemison, Mae **222–223**, 223
Jerusalem 27–28
Jesuits 34, 35
Jewelry **4**, **62–63**, 231, **231**
Jim Crow laws 111, 129, 161
Johnson, Marguerite see Angelou, Maya
Johnson, Richard M. (U.S. Vice Pres.)
    78, **78–79**
Jordan, Barbara **190**, 191

Kebra Negast 27, 28
Keckley, Elizabeth 105, **105**, 107–108
Keckley, George 105
Kelly, Sharon Pratt 206, 207, **207**
Kennedy, John F. (U.S. Pres.) 167, 174
Kente cloth **16**, 17
Kentucky: slaves 116
Kenya: women **2–3**, **208–209**, 209
Keys, Alicia 242, **244**
Kikuyu **2–3**
Kiluanji, King (Ndongo) 34
King, Coretta Scott 154, **168**, 169, 190,
    192–193, 193–196
King, Martin Luther, Jr. 161, **168**, 175,
    177, 184, 191, 194, 224
King, Rodney 206
Kulibali, Amina 31
Kush, Kingdom of, Africa 25; iconogra-
    phy 28, **29**
KwaZulu-Natal (region), southern
    Africa 34–35

Laney, Lucy Craft 149
Langeni people 35–36
Lawson, Jesse 144
Lincoln, Abraham (U.S. Pres.) 108
Lincoln, Mary Todd 105, 107–108
Lincoln, Robert 107
Lincoln Memorial, Washington, D.C.
    162, **163**, 164, 166
"Lineage" (Alexander) 71
Los Angeles, California 111, 116, 200,
    204, 205
Louisiana 154, **156–157**, 166; slaves
    76–77, 88, 135
Lynchings 118, 122, 129, 136, 146, 161

M Street High School, Washington,
    D.C. 137, 141, 144, 146
Machel, Graça 214, **216–217**, 240–242
Madega of Dogomba, King 28–29, 31
Maine Anti-Slavery Society 104
Makeda, Queen of Sheba (Ethiopia)
    27–28, 28, 47
Mali: royalty 28; women **40–41**, 43
Mandela, Nelson 214, **216**, 242
Manillas 52, **52**
Mann, Horace: quoted 194
Maroons 56–57, 60, 73
Marriage: certificate **106**, 107; inter-
    racial 77, 78, 91
Marshall, Thurgood 177, 207
Martin Luther King, Jr., Center for
    Nonviolent Social Change 195
Maryland: slaves 101, 104
Mason, Bridget "Biddy" 111, 116
Massachusetts: free Blacks 130; slaves
    77, **77**, 82, 109; witchcraft 73–74, 76
Massaleke Kingdom, Senegal 30–31
Matamba (region), Africa 35
Mbandi 34, 35
Mbundu 34
Medal of Honor 164, 176
Memphis, Tennessee 121–122, 144, 146,
    195
Mende 233
Menilek 28
Metoyer, Claude 76–77
Mexico: stone head **19**
Michigan: Blacks **152**, 153
Migrations: early humans 18–19; north-
    ward 143, 161, 182; westward 108–112,
    115–116, 120
Military: Blacks in 92, 133, 167, 210, **211**
Million Woman March (1997) 236,
    237–238
Mills, Loren 200
Miner, Myrtilla 91
Minority Women Employment
    Program 213
Miss Black America Pageant **180–181**,
    181
Mississippi: slaves 121; voter registra-
    tion 178, 182
Missouri 105, 116, 135, 144

Mitanni, Kingdom of, Africa 26–27
Montana 117
Montana Territory 112
Montgomery, Ala.: bus boycotts 164,
    174–176, 194
Monticello, Va. 77, 80–81
Moran, Mary **232**, 233
Morejón, Nancy **58**, 59
Morrison, Toni 225, **226–227**, 227
Moseley-Braun, Carol **188–189**, 191,
    210–211, 213
Moss, Tom 146
Mossi Kingdom, West Africa 31
Mother Clubs 147
Motown Records 182
Mozambique 240–242
Mtetwa people 36
Mulattoes 64–66, 76–78, 80–81
Murray, Pauli: quoted 99
Music 121, 233; performers 161–162, **163**,
    164–165, 182, **183**, 202, **202–203**, 230,
    231, 242, **244–245**

"Nananbouclou and the Piece of Fire"
    (folktale): quote 14
Nandi 35–36
Nanny, Queen of the Maroons 56–57,
    57, 60, 73
Napata, Kingdom of 24
National American Woman Suffrage
    Association 146
National Association for the Advance-
    ment of Colored People (NAACP)
    122, 129, 130, 133, 136, 149, 174–177, 194,
    196, 225
National Association of Colored
    Women (NACW) 105, 146–147
National Colored Women's Congress
    105
National Council of Negro Women
    (NCNW) 154, 166, 182, 184, 225, 228, 231
National Council of Women 147
National Negro Business League 136
National Political Congress for Black
    Women 200
National Women's Political Caucus
    200
Native Americans **90**, 91; see also Black
    Indians
Ndongo (present-day Angola) 34–35
Nebraska: Blacks 112, **112**, **114–115**, 115
New Orleans, La.: segregation 166, **167**;
    slaves 88
New York: Blacks **126–127**, 129, 143, 197,
    218–219, 221
Nigeria 52
Nightingale, Florence 66
Nobel Prize 225, 227
Nonviolent protests 194, 195
North Carolina: slaves 137
North (region), U.S.: Black migrants to
    142–143, 143, 161, 182; see also states by
    name

Nubians 17, 20, **24**, 25–26, **27**, 28
Nzinga, Anna de Sousa, Queen 34, 43

Oberlin College, Ohio 91, 136, 137, 140, 146, 235
Ohio 101, 104, 107, 117, 191
Olmec: stone head **19**
On to Liberty (painting) **84–85**, 85
The Oprah Winfrey Show 230
Osburn, Sarah 74
Ouedraogo 29, 31

Pakistan: bronze figurine **18**
Pan-African Conference 141
Parks, Rosa Marie McCauley 164, **164**, 165, 174–176, 177, 187, 194
Parris, Elizabeth 74
Parris, Samuel 74, 76
Patterson, Mary Saunders 162
Pearl (ship) 88, 91
Pennsylvania Freedman's Relief Association 93
Philadelphia, Pa.: Blacks 93, 143, 162, 170, 236, **236–237**
Philadelphia Female Anti-Slavery Society 93
Philanthropists 136, 231, 234
Phips, William 74
Pleasant, John James 109, 110
Pleasant, Mary Ellen 109–111
Plessy v. Ferguson 161, 175–176
Porgy and Bess (opera) 224
Port Royal Experiment 93
Portuguese: slave trade 34, 43, 47, 52
Powell, Colin 238, **238**
Presidency, U.S.: Black candidates **194**, 195, 200, 213
Presidential Medal of Freedom 176, 184
Prince, Dinah 61, 64
Prince, Hannah 61, 64
Prince, Mary 61, 64
Princeton Univ., Princeton, N.J. 238–239
Pringle, Rachel **60**, 61
Pulitzer Prize 225, 227
Purvis, Robert 82
Purvis family 93
Putnam, Ann 74

Quadroons 81
Quakers 82, 109; diary 88, **89**

Race riots 161, 200, 204, 205
Raile, Prince (Mali) 29
Random House Books 228
Reagan, Ronald (U.S. Pres.) 184
Reconstruction 93, 130, 132
Reese, James 200
Religion 43, 52, 55, 99; baptism **98–99**; see also Catholicism; Yoruba cult
Renaissance Noir 221

Reynolds, Barbara 169
Rice, Condoleezza **238**, 239–240
Robinson, JoAnn 176
Roosevelt, Eleanor 162, 177, 182
Roosevelt, Franklin D. (U.S. Pres.) 154
Rousseau, Henri: painting **14–15**, 17
Royalty: Egypt, ancient 17, 20–21, **22**, 23–27, **27**, 28, **29**; Ethiopia 27–28, 47; Ghana 28–29, 31; Senegal 31
Rudolph, Wilma 170, **170**, **171**
"Ruth" (Murray) 99

Saint James, Synthia 240, **241**
São Tomé, Brazil: slave trading fort 52
Scarab, jade **26**
Scarring, ritual **62–63**
Schools: desegregation 149; interracial 93; segregated 93, 166, 175–176; see also Citizenship schools; schools by name
Scotia Seminary for Colored Girls, Concord, North Carolina 149
Scott, Coretta see King, Coretta Scott
Sea Islands, Ga.–S.C. 91, 92–94, 177–178
Seacole, Mary 64–65, **65**, 66
Sedeinga, Nubia: temple 26
Segregation 93, 121, 147, 149, 161, 164, 165, 169, 173, 179, 184, 191; see also Buses: boycotts; Schools: segregated
Selma, Alabama: Civil Rights march **158–59**, 161
Senegal: royalty 31; slave trade 47
Senmut 20–21, 25
Senzangakhoma (Zulu chief) 35
Serers tribe 31
Sexual harassment: workplace 200, 206–207, 210
Shaka (Zulu) 35–36
Sharecroppers 103, 179, 238
Sheba, Queen of (Ethiopia) 27–28, 47
"She's Free!" (Harper) 97
Shores family 112, **112**
Sierra Leone 233; slaves 47, 92
Simmons, Ruth 238–239
Simpson, Georgiana R. 144
Singleton, Benjamin "Pap" 111; poster **111**
Sisulu, Sheila 240
Slave ships 48, 49, 50, 51, 52, 56
Slave trade 34, 43, 45, 49–51; by Africans 34, 43, 47, 52; forts 47, **48–49**, 49, 50; markets **44–45**, 45, 47, 51, 61, 64, 231
Slaves **72**, 74, 75, **75**, 169, 174, 230, 231; Alabama 108; badges 74, **74**; bracelets 52, **52**; clothing 52, **53**; freed 91, 94, **95–96**, 100, **100**, 107, 116–117, 139, 197; Louisiana 135; North Carolina 137; property book 74, **75**; runaways 56–57, 60, 81–83, 83, **84–85**, 85, **86**, 88, **88**, 91, 110; songs 233; Tennessee 117, 144; torture 82, **83**; Virginia 116; see also Abolitionists; Antislavery movement; Underground Railroad
Smith, Alexander 109

Smith, James 81
Smith, Rebecca 111
Smith, Robert 111
Solomon, King (Jerusalem) 27–28
Song of Solomon (Bible) 27
Sororities 130, 154, **156–157**, 166, 171, 184
South Africa 242; apartheid 176, 196, 205, 240; women 66, **67**
South America: slaves 43, 45, 51, 73; see also Brazil
South Carolina 149, 152, 176–178; abolitionists 94; slaves 92
South (region), U.S.: lynchings 118, 122, 146, 129; slavery 9, 73, 81, 82, 91; see also states by name
Southern Christian Leadership Conference 178, 195, 224–225
Spelman College, Atlanta, Ga. 136, 164, **196**, 197, 234, 235, 238, 239
St. Augustine's Normal School, Raleigh, N.C. 137
St. Luke, Independent Order of 132–133, 135
St. Luke Penny Savings Bank, Richmond, Va. 133, **133**
Stanton, Elizabeth Cady 104
Stewart-Lai, Carlotta 122, **123**
Still, William 82, 101
Stowe, Harriet Beecher 91
Student Nonviolent Coordinating Committee (SNCC) 174, 179
Suffrage movement 101, 104, 122, 146, 147, 149; see also Voting rights
Sultane (slave ship) 51
Supreme Court, U.S. 164, 175–176, 184, 200, 206–207, 210, 211
Surinam: women 52, **53**

Talented Tenth 129–130, 144
Tamrin, Prince 27
Tanner, Benjamin Tucker 170
Tattler Girls Athletic and Social Club 149, **149**
Taylor, Susie Baker King 91–92, 94, **95**
Tennessee 144, 146, 170, **171**, 177, 195, 202; slaves 117
Terrell, Mary Church 130, 131, 137, **138**, 139–140, 144, 146–147, 149, 184, **185**; quoted 127
Terrell, Robert Heberton 146
Textiles **4**, 11
Thomas, Clarence 200, 206–207, 210
Thomas (slave ship) 51
13th Amendment 101, 129
Thutmose I, Pharaoh (Egypt) 17, 20
Thutmose II, Pharaoh (Egypt) 17, 20
Thutmose III, Pharaoh (Egypt) 20, 25
Tiye, Queen (Egypt) 25–26, **27**, 28
"To a Dark Girl" (Bennett) 41
"To Black Women" (Brooks) 124
Triangular trade see Slave trade
Truman, Harry S., (U.S. Pres.) 167, 174

Truth, Sojourner **86**, 87
Tubman, Harriet 88, 94
Tukulor tribe 31
Turner, Tina 202, **202–203**
Tushratta, King of Mittani 26–27

Uncle Tom's Cabin (Stowe) 91
Underground Railroad 82, 85, 88, **89**, 92, 94, 101, 109
Utah: slaves 111

Virginia 132, 166; slaves 73, 74, 75, 77, 80–81, 116
Voter registration 177–178, 184
Voting rights 161, 166, 174, 182, 209; see also Suffrage movement
Voting Rights Act (1965) 182

Walker, Armstead 132
Walker, Charles Joseph 135
Walker, Madam C. J. **134**, 135, **135**, 136, 228
Walker, Maggie Lena 132–133, **133**, 135–136
Washington, Booker T. 130, 136, 144, 149, 153
Washington, D.C. 108, 162, **163**, 164, 166; Blacks 166, **206**, 207, **207**; civil rights rallies 179, **179**, 184, 195; free blacks 105, 107; schools **128**, 129, 137, 141, 144, 146, 165; slaves 83, 88, 91, 105, 231
Washington, Denzel **220**, 221
Washington, Harold 210
Waters, Edward 204, 205
Waters, Maxine 204–206
Watkins, Frances Ellen see Harper, Frances Ellen Watkins
Watts riots 200, 204
Wayles, John 77
Wells-Barnett, Ida B. **118**, 119, 121–122
West (region), U.S.: Black migrants 108–112, **112–115**, 115–116, 120; see also states by name
Wheatley, Phyllis: poetry book **76**, 77
Wilberforce University, Ohio 101, 107, 130, 136, 146
Wilkins, Roy 184
Williams, Abigail 74
Williams, Betsey 61
Williams, Fannie Barrier 141
Williams, Hosea 178
Williams, Vanessa L. 181
Wilson, Emma J. 149
Windward Maroons 56–57, 60, 73
Winfrey, Oprah 228–231, **229**, 242
Witchcraft 73–74, 76
Wolof tribe 31
Women warriors **32–33**, 33, 34
Women's Bureau, U.S. Dept. of Labor 213–214

Women's Political Council (WPC) 176
Women's rights **87**, 130, 133, 146, 206, 235
World Health Assembly, Geneva,
 Switzerland 167
World War II 133, 161; Blacks workers
 153, **153**
World's Congress of Representative
 Women (1875) 104–105, 141

Yemanjá (deity) 52, 56
Yennenga of West Africa 28–29, 31
Yoruba cult 52, 55, 56
Young, Andrew 178, 195
Young, Whitney 184
Young Women's Christian Association
 (YWCA) 135, 167, 182, 184
Yuya 25

Zanzibar: slave trade **44–45,** 45
Zulu clan 35–36

illustrations credits

Cover, "Precious" © 1996 SAINT JAMES/BIBBS. A Mixed Media Painting Collaboration between Synthia SAINT JAMES and Charles BIBBS; inside flap-dust jacket courtesy Cynthia Jacobs Carter, Karl W. Carter, Jr., photographer.

2-3, Carl & Ann Purcell/CORBIS; 4, Bruce Dale; 9, Betty Kleckley Stradford, courtesy National Council of Negro Women, Inc.; 10, Nik Wheeler/CORBIS; 12-13, © 2000 by Michael Cunningham and Craig Marberry/Agent, Victoria Sanders & Associates; 14-15, Lauros/Giraudon/Bridgeman Art Library; 16, CORBIS; 18, James P. Blair; 19, Kenneth Garrett; 21, Kazuyoshi Nomachi; 22, Gianni Dagli Orti/CORBIS; 24, Werner Forman/Art Resource; 26, Louvre, Paris, France/Giraudon/Bridgeman Art Library; 27, Werner Foreman/Art Resource; 29, Enrico Ferorelli; 30, Musee de l'Oeuvre de Notre Dame, Strasbourg, France/Bridgeman Art Library; 32-33, University of Virginia Special Collections Library, Alderman Library; 33, Frederick E. Forbes, Dahomey and the Dahomans: being the journals of two missions to the King of Dahomey, and the residence in his capital, in 1849 and 1850 (London, 1851), Vol. 1; 37, © Dirk Bakker 1980 ; 38-39, David Coulson/Robert Estall agency; 40-41, Jose Azel/AURORA; 42, Moorland-Spingarn Research Center/Howard University; 44-45, Bojan Brecelj/CORBIS; 46, Giraudon/Bridgeman Art Library; 48-49, Gordon Gahan/NG Image Collection; 48, courtesy The Library of Congress; 52, Sample Noel Pittman Collection/Schomburg Center; 54-55, Stephanie Maze/CORBIS; 54-55, Peter Harholdt/CORBIS; 57, Bank of Jamiaca; 58, courtesy of Michael B. Smith; 60, Barbados Museum and Historical Society; 62-63, courtesy of the John Carter Brown Library at Brown University; 65, Gustav LeGray/The J. Paul Getty Museum; 67, City of Westminster Archive Center, London/Bridgeman Art Library; 68-69, Moorland-Spingarn Research Center/Howard University; 70-71, Los Angeles County Museum of Art, Acquisition made possible through Museum Trustees: Robert O. Anderson, R. Stanton Avery, B. Gerald Cantor, Edward W. Carter, Justin Dart, Charles E. Ducommun, Camilla Chadler Frost, Julian Ganz, Jr., Dr. Armand Hammer, Harry Lenart, Dr. Franklin D. Murphy, Joan Palevsky, Richard E. Sherwood, Maynard J. Toll, and Hal B. Wallis; 72, originally published in "The Liberator" on January 7, 1832.; 74, Schomburg Center; 75 (background), J.T. Zealy, 1850. Peabody Museum, Harvard University; 75 (foreground), North Hampton Circuit Court; 76, MARB/Schomburg Center; 77, Massachusetts Historical Society; 78-79, The Library Company of Philadelphia; 80, Moorland-Spingarn Research Center/Howard University; 83, courtesy The Library of Congress, LC USZ62 43972; 84-85, Private Collection/Bridgeman Art Library; 86, National Portrait Gallery, Smithsonian Institution; 88, Jim Gensheimer/NG Image Collection; 89, From the Manigault Papers, #484, Southern Historical Collection, The Library of the University of North Carolina, Chapel Hill; 90, Western History Collection, University of Oklahoma, Norman, Frank Phillips Collection, photo #975; 95, Moorland-Spingarn Research Center/Howard University; 96-97, Gladstone Collection; 98-99, Doris Ulmann, courtesy David Featherstone; 100, The Historic New Orleans Collection; 102-103, George Eastman House; 104, Moorland-Spingarn Research Center/Howard University; 105, Moorland-Spingarn Research Center/Howard University; 106 (background), Schomburg Center; 106 (inset), reprinted with permission of Russell & Volkening as agents for the author. Copyright 1999 by Jackie Napolean Wilson; 109, courtesy The Library of Congress, LC USZ62 104928; 110, The Miriam Matthews Collection; 111, courtesy The Library of Congress LC USZ62 120006; 112, Nebraska State His-

torical Society; 113, Ursuline Convent Offices; 114-115, Nebraska State Historical Society; 118, courtesy The Library of Congress LC USZ62 107756; 120, Hulton-Deutsch Collection/CORBIS; 123, Moorland-Spingarn Research Center/Howard University; 124-125, Moorland-Spingarn Research Center/Howard University; 126-127, "Photograph by Austin Hansen used by permission of Joyce Hansen and The Schomburg Center."; 128, Francis Benjamin Johnston/CORBIS; 131 (background), courtesy The Library of Congress; 132, courtesy Andrew C. Blair; 133, Valentine Richmond History Center; 134, Schomburg Center; 135, Madam C. J. Walker Collection, R1373, Indiana Historical Society; 138, Moorland-Spingarn Research Center/Howard University; 140, Florida State Archives; 141, Moorland-Spingarn Research Center/Howard University; 142, courtesy The Library of Congress; 142-143, Jack Delano/CORBIS; 145 (background), Los Angeles Public Library; 145 (foreground), Security Pacific Collection/Los Angeles Public Library; 147, Moorland-Spingarn Research Center/Howard University; 148, The family of Selma Beck Harry and Girl Scouts of Hoosier Capital Council; 149, Schomburg Center; 150-151, From the Mugar Memorial Library Collection in the Special Collections at Boston University; 152, courtesy Detroit Public Library, Burton Historical Collection; 153, Gordon Parks/CORBIS; 155, Gordon Parks/CORBIS; 156-157, courtesy Cynthia Jacobs Carter; 158-159, Charles Moore/BLACK STAR; 160, Donald Uhrbrook/Time Life Pictures/Getty Images; 163, Bettmann/CORBIS; 164, Gene Herrick/AP/Wide World Photos; 165, Bettmann/CORBIS; 167 (upper), AP/Wide World Photos; 168, Charles Moore/BLACK STAR; 170, Bettmann/CORBIS; 171, Getty Images; 172-173, Bettmann/CORBIS; 175 (upper), AP/Wide World Photos; 178, AP/Wide World Photos; 179, AP/Wide World Photos; 180-181, Hulton Archives/Getty Images; 182, David J. and Janice L. Frent Collection/CORBIS; 183, Bettmann/CORBIS; 185, Moorland-Spingarn Research Center/Howard University; 186-187, Bettmann/CORBIS; 188-189, Reuters NewsMedia Inc./CORBIS; 190, AP/Wide World Photos; 192-193, Flip Schulke/CORBIS; 194, Owen Franken/CORBIS; 196, courtesy of Spelman College Archives, Atlanta, Georgia; 197, courtesy of Spelman College Archives, Atlanta, Georgia; 198, Brian Lanker; 201, Mark Leighton/Bettmann/CORBIS; 202-203, Michel Euler/AP/Wide World Photos; 206, Wally McNamee/CORBIS; 207, Wally McNamee/CORBIS; 208-209, AP/Wide World Photos; 211, David Turnley/CORBIS; 212, Brian Lanker; 215, Paul Kolnik/Alvin Ailey's American Dance Theater; 216-217, AFP/CORBIS; 218-219, Stone Les/CORBIS Sygma; 220, Mark J. Terrill/AP/Wide World Photos; 222-223, NASA STS047 37 003; 224, Mark Lennihan/AP/Wide World Photos; 226-227, AP/Wide World Photos; 229, Getty Images; 230, Stuart Ramson/AP/Wide World Photos; 231, Breton Littlehales; 232, INKO Producciones S. L.; 236-237, AFP/Getty Images; 238, Sean Gallup/Getty Images; 241, Leroy Hamilton; 243, Getty Images; 244-245, Obed Zilwa/AP/Wide World Photos; 246, Sharon Reese, "Ndebele Lady."

africana woman
HER STORY THROUGH TIME

Dr. Cynthia Jacobs Carter
Introduction by Dr. Dorothy Height

Published by the National Geographic Society

John M. Fahey, Jr., *President and Chief Executive Officer*
Gilbert M. Grosvenor, *Chairman of the Board*
Nina D. Hoffman, *Executive Vice President*

Prepared by the Book Division

Kevin Mulroy, *Vice President and Editor-in-Chief*
Charles Kogod, *Illustrations Director*
Marianne R. Koszorus, *Design Director*
Barbara Brownell Grogan, *Executive Editor*

Staff for this Book

Jane Sunderland, *Editor*
Susan Blair, *Illustrations Editor*
Cinda Rose, *Art Director*
Donna M. Wells, *Researcher*
Marilyn Mobley McKenzie, *Consultant*
Carl Mehler, *Director of Maps*
Matt Chwastyk, *Map Research*
Sarah Evans, *Contributing Writer*
Susan Tyler Hitchcock, *Contributing Editor*
Margo Browning, *Contributing Editor*
Gary Colbert, *Production Director*
Lewis Bassford, *Production Project Manager*
Janet Dustin, *Illustrations Assistant*
Theodore Tucker, *Design Assistant*

Manufacturing and Quality Control

Christopher A. Liedel, *Chief Financial Officer*
Phillip L. Schlosser, *Managing Director*
John T. Dunn, *Technical Director*

Library of Congress Cataloging-in-Publication Data

Carter, Cynthia Jacobs.
Africana woman: her story through time / Dr. Cynthia Jacobs Carter; introduction by Dr. Dorothy Height.

p. cm.

Includes bibliographical references and index.
ISBN 0-7922-6165-8 (alk. paper)
African American women—History. 2. African American women—Biography. 3. Women, Black—History. 4. Women, Black—Biography. I. Title.

E185.86.C325 2003
305.48'96—dc21

2003056168

One of the world's largest nonprofit scientific and educational organizations, the National Geographic Society was founded in 1888 "for the increase and diffusion of geographic knowledge." Fulfilling this mission, the Society educates and inspires millions every day through its magazines, books, television programs, videos, maps and atlases, research grants, the National Geographic Bee, teacher workshops, and innovative classroom materials. The Society is supported through membership dues, charitable gifts, and income from the sale of its educational products. This support is vital to National Geographic's mission to increase global understanding and promote conservation of our planet through exploration, research, and education.

For more information, please call 1-800-NGS LINE (647-5463) or write to the following address:

National Geographic Society
1145 17th Street N.W.
Washington, D.C. 20036-4688 U.S.A.

Visit the Society's Web site at
www.nationalgeographic.com.